CONTEMPORARY'S

GED

SOCIAL STUDIES EXERCISE BOOK

Kenneth Tamarkin

Jeri W. Bayer

D1596472

McGraw-Hill
Contemporary

Development Editor: Anne Petti Smith
Executive Editor: Linda Kwil
Creative Director: Michael E. Kelly
Marketing Manager: Sean Klunder
Production Manager: Genevieve Kelley
Manager of Editorial Services: Sylvia Bace

McGraw-Hill/Contemporary

A Division of The McGraw-Hill Companies

Send all inquiries to:

Wright Group/McGraw-Hill
130 E. Randolph, Suite 400
Chicago, IL 60601

ISBN: 0-8092-2234-5

Printed in the United States of America.

7 8 9 10 QWD 09

Table of Contents

Acknowledgments

Excerpt on page 4 from "Remembering Crash of '29" by Tom Tiede, *The News-Sun,* Oct. 24–25, 1987. Reprinted by permission of Tom Tiede and Newspaper Enterprise Association.

Excerpt on page 7 from *Mothers Who Work: Strategies for Coping,* by Jeanne Bodin and Bonnie Mitelman. Copyright © 1983 by Jeanne Bodin and Bonnie Mitelman. Reprinted by permission of Ballantine Books, a Division of Random House, Inc.

Excerpt on page 11 from "The Centrist Doesn't Hold" by Margaret Carlson, *Time,* June 4, 2001. © 2001 Time Inc. Reprinted with permission.

Excerpt on page 12 from "Russia Stalled" by Timothy J. Colton, as appeared in *Harvard* Magazine, March-April 1999. Reprinted by permission of Timothy J. Colton, Professor of Government, Harvard University.

Excerpt on page 17 from review by Arch Puddington. Reprinted from *Commentary,* October 2000, by permission; all rights reserved.

Cartoon on page 18 by Steve Breen/Copley News Service.

Photo on page 18 by J. R. Eyerman/TimePix.

Excerpt on page 19 from "Spring Comes Early to Silicon Valley" by Michael Moritz, *Time,* August 26, 2001. © 2001 Time Inc. Reprinted with permission.

Painting on page 19 by Archibald Willard, *The Spirit of '76.*

Photo on page 20 by Mansell/TimePix.

Excerpt on page 21 from *Bury My Heart at Wounded Knee* by Dee Brown, © 1970 by Henry Holt and Co. Reprinted by permission of Henry Holt & Co., LLC.

Map on page 22 from *Maps On File* by Martin Greenwald Associates. Copyright © 1985 by Martin Greenwald Associates. Reprinted by permission of Facts On File, Inc.

Cartoon on page 24 © Tribune Media Services, Inc. All Rights Reserved. Reprinted with permission.

Map on page 26 from the book *The First Book Atlas,* edited by Hammond Incorporated. Copyright © 1960 by Hammond Incorporated. Reprinted with permission of Grolier Publishing Company.

Table on page 27 from *North to Aztlán: A History of Mexican Americans in the U.S.* by Richard Griswold del Castillo & Arnoldo De Leon. © 1996 Twayne Publishers. Reprinted by permission of The Gale Group.

Column, "Southwest, Males", in table on page 27 from *The Chicano Worker* by Vernon M. Briggs, Jr., Walter Fogel, and Fred Schmidt. Copyright © 1977. Courtesy of the University of Texas Press.

Excerpt on page 28 from "Toxic Wastes and The New World Order" by Mitchel Cohen as appeared in *Synthesis/Regeneration,* a magazine of the Green Party, USA. Reprinted by permission of the author.

Photo on page 29 by Loomis Dean/TimePix.

Excerpt on page 31 reprinted with permission from Microsoft Corporation as made available through Microsoft® Encarta® Encyclopedia 2001.

Photo of prisoners working on page 31 © Bettmann/CORBIS.

Photo of solitary confinement cells on page 31 © Bettmann/CORBIS.

Cartoon on page 34 © Tribune Media Services, Inc. All Rights Reserved. Reprinted with permission.

Excerpt on page 35 from "The Gaza Strip: An Interview with Alexandra Avakian" as appeared on www.nationalgeographic.com. Reprinted by permission of Alexandra Avakian.

Excerpt on page 36 from "Building a Neighborhood," from *A Home in the Heart of the City* by Kathleen Hirsch. Copyright © 1998 by Kathleen Hirsch. Reprinted by permission of Farrar, Straus and Giroux, LLC.

Cartoon on page 37 from Pearson/Rothco.

Excerpt on page 39 from *The Making of the President 1960* by Theodore H. White. Reprinted by permission of Theodore H. White.

Chart on page 40 from "Speech That Should Be Restricted," Center for Survey Research and Analysis, 1997. Reprinted by permission.

Excerpt on page 40 from "Freedom of Expression," Briefing Paper Number 10, 1997. Copyright © 1997, American Civil Liberties Union. Reprinted with permission of the American Civil Liberties Union.

Photo on page 45 from CULVER PICTURES.

Excerpt on page 45 reprinted with permission from Microsoft Corporation as made available through Microsoft® Encarta® Encyclopedia 2001.

Excerpt on page 45 from *Politics, Power, and People* by Thomas Raynor. Copyright © 1983 by Thomas Raynor. Reprinted by permission of Grolier Publishing Co.

Photo on page 49 from Brown Brothers.

Excerpt on page 51 from *Native American Rights* by Tamara L. Roleff.

Excerpt on page 52 reprinted with the permission of Simon & Schuster from *The Wrath of Nations: Civilization and the Furies of Nationalism* by William Pfaff. Copyright © 1993 by William Pfaff.

Chart on page 65, "Douglas Aircraft Co., Selected Statistics, 1939–1944" from *The Entrepeneurs* by Robert Sobel, 1974. Reprinted by permission of Beard Books.

Cartoons on page 66 by Mike Keefe, dePIXion studios. Reprinted by permission.

Chart on page 69 from *IT and the New Economy: Macro, Jobs, and Gender* by J. Bernstein, 2000. Economic Policy Institute, Washington, DC. Reprinted by permission.

Excerpt and graph on page 92, "We all live on the Exxon Valdez," reprinted with permission from the March/April 1999 issue of *Sierra.*

Excerpt on page 93 from "The Rise of the NAFTA Manager," *Time,* June 11, 2001. © 2001 Time Inc. Reprinted with permission.

Excerpt on page 94 from "Future Harvest" by Lisa Rao, as appeared in *Calypso Log* Magazine, April 1999, published by the Cousteau Society, Inc. Reprinted by permission of the author.

Photo of East Berlin on page 95 from Associated Press/AP.

Photo of demonstration on page 95 by Stanley Forman/Boston Herald/American.

Photo of Brasilia on page 96 © Bettmann/CORBIS.

Photo of refugee camp on page 96 © AFP/CORBIS.

Excerpt on page 97 from "The Politics of Forgetting" by Tim Ledwith, from *Amnesty Action,* Spring 1999. Reprinted by permission of Amnesty International U.S.A.

Cartoon on page 98 from Raeside/Rothco.

Photo on page 98 by Greg Gibson/Associated Press.

Excerpt on page 99 from "How the U.S. Capitol, a lofty symbol of national confidence, can also cheer a weary heart" by Dwight Young. From *Preservation,* The Magazine of the National Trust for Historic Preservation, March-April 1999. Reprinted by permission.

Photo on page 99 © Joseph Sohm, Visions of America/CORBIS.

Photo of China on page 102 from UN/DPI Photo.

Photo of camels on page 102 © George Steinmetz.

Cartoon on page 103 from Liederman/Rothco.

Excerpt on page 105 from "Asia Eyes Radical Alternatives to Gasoline" by Godwin Chellam. Copyright © 2001 Reuters. Reprinted with permission.

Cartoon on page 106 by John Spencer. Reprinted with permission of Philadelphia Business Journal.

Cartoon on page 110 from CULVER PICTURES.

Photo on page 114 from Associated Press/AP.

Photo on page 125 © Bettmann/CORBIS.

Introduction

Welcome to Contemporary's *GED Social Studies Exercise Book.* The purpose of this book is to provide you with additional practice in answering the types of questions that will appear on the actual GED Social Studies Test. The organization of this book parallels Part II of the book *GED Social Studies,* Themes in Social Studies, so if you need more in-depth review or further instruction, refer to the pages from that book listed at the beginning of each chapter. The pages listed from Contemporary's *Complete GED* will also give further instruction and practice.

Like Contemporary's *GED Social Studies* and the GED Social Studies Test, this book covers the following content areas and critical thinking skills in the percentages in which they appear on the test:

Content Area

World History	15%
U.S. History	25%
Civics and Government	25%
Economics	20%
Geography	15%

Critical Thinking Skills

Comprehension	20%
Application	20%
Analysis	40%
Evaluation	20%

Content

In order to practice the content-area skills, you will find many reading passages taken from original sources that provide information about the content areas listed above. In addition to reading passages, there are many visuals in this book, such as charts, maps, graphs, photographs, and cartoons. Visuals such as these make up over 50% of the 2002 GED Test, and the exercises in this book will help to prepare you for questions based on these types of graphics. At the end of the book, a complete Answer Key provides the correct answer and explains why the other answers are not correct. It also indicates which critical thinking skill is being tested in each question.

Practice Test

After completing the exercises in this book, we recommend that you take the Practice Test at the end of the book to determine whether you are ready to take the GED Social Studies Test. The Practice Test contains 50 multiple-choice questions, the same number of questions as you will find on the actual test. Since you will have 70 minutes to complete the actual GED test, we recommend that you try to complete the Practice Test in 70 minutes as well. This will give you an idea of how well you would do on the actual test.

Evaluation and Further Practice

To help you pinpoint the areas in which you need additional practice, an Evaluation Chart is provided after the Practice Test. This chart identifies each question on the Practice Test according to the content area and critical thinking skill that is being tested. For additional practice, you can refer to *Contemporary's GED Social Studies* or *Contemporary's Complete GED,* both of which devote an entire chapter to each of the skills necessary to pass the GED Social Studies Test. At the beginning of each section of this exercise book, you will see page references which refer you to the pages in these books where the skills covered in that chapter can be found.

Chapter 1

Time, Continuity, and Change

GED Social Studies pages 119–156
Complete GED pages 297–326, 427–443

Questions 1–3 are based on the following map.

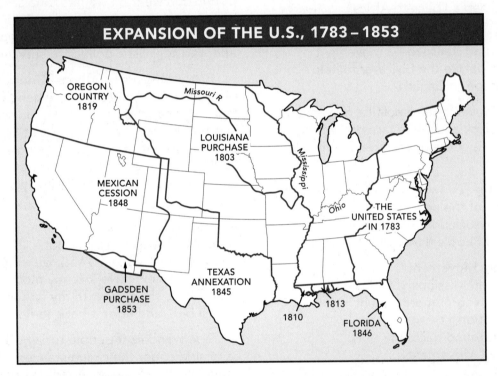

EXPANSION OF THE U.S., 1783–1853

OREGON COUNTRY 1819

Missouri R

LOUISIANA PURCHASE 1803

Mississippi

MEXICAN CESSION 1848

Ohio

THE UNITED STATES IN 1783

GADSDEN PURCHASE 1853

TEXAS ANNEXATION 1845

1813

1810

FLORIDA 1846

1. Which of the following states was not part of the United States in 1783?

    (1) New York
    (2) Virginia
    (3) Florida
    (4) Georgia
    (5) South Carolina

2. Under which of the following was California brought within the borders of the United States?

    (1) the Oregon Country Settlement
    (2) the Mexican Cession
    (3) the Gadsden Purchase
    (4) the Texas Annexation
    (5) the Louisiana Purchase

3. Which of the following national moods resulted most directly from the Louisiana Purchase?

    (1) a demand that foreign powers not interfere in the Americas
    (2) an intense desire for further territorial expansion
    (3) strong loyalty to one's native region above all others
    (4) the belief that Americans must care for the less fortunate countries
    (5) a belief in the need to maintain good relations with other nations

Questions 4 and 5 are based on the following terms.

Niagara Movement—a movement to end discrimination and segregation in the United States

American Missionary Association—a movement of Christian teachers who went south after the Civil War to volunteer their teaching services

United Negro Improvement Association—a separatist movement of black Americans who launched a "back to Africa" movement

Underground Railroad—a movement organized before the Civil War to help slaves escape to Canada

Populist Movement—a political movement in which black and white farmers united to try to overcome oppressive conditions

4. Which of the following was most likely a forerunner of the advocacy group the National Association for the Advancement of Colored People (NAACP)?

   (1) Niagara Movement
   (2) American Missionary Association
   (3) United Negro Improvement Association
   (4) Underground Railroad
   (5) Populist Movement

5. Which of the following could have been described as the "early American Peace Corps"?

   (1) Niagara Movement
   (2) American Missionary Association
   (3) United Negro Improvement Association
   (4) Underground Railroad
   (5) Populist Movement

Questions 6–9 are based on the following passage about the Great Depression.

Sipe was a young dairy farmer in Kansas at the time. He was land rich and apparently secure by the standards of the day, and then the stock market crashed in October 1929; he was wiped out by the worldwide depression that followed. . . .

Agnes Gellan of Fargo, N.D., says that two-thirds of the banks in that state closed during the turmoil, and a third of the population went on welfare. She says 90,000 people fled the state to seek relief in other places, and many of those who stayed adopted socialistic politics to survive.

Bruce Medaris of Athens, Georgia, was between military enlistments when the market failed. He says he had $100,000 in securities and no idea they were in any particular danger. He says he lost everything except $100, "and I spent that on a suit of clothes, so I could begin my new life in style."

And Dellie Norton of Canton, N.C. She was raised in Appalachia, where prosperity went instantly from little to none. "I remember one Christmas we gave each other an apple. A single apple. I gave it to my mother who took a bite, she gave it to my father, who took a bite, and I got it back to finish. . . ."

Sipe wonders if people today would be as pliable under the circumstances. The others I've interviewed wonder as well. They think Americans of the 1930s were "a more formidable breed," as Sipe puts it. They were raised on adversities, and they had the psychological skills to cope with terrible change.

6. Which of the following is an opinion expressed by one of the survivors of the Great Depression?

   (1) "He was land rich and apparently secure by the standards of the day."
   (2) "Many of those who stayed adopted socialistic politics to survive."
   (3) "I lost everything except $100, and I spent that on a suit of clothes."
   (4) "Prosperity went instantly from little to none."
   (5) "Americans of the 1930s were 'a more formidable breed.'"

7. What was the most direct cause of the worldwide depression described in this passage?

   (1) the adoption of socialistic politics by many Americans
   (2) the closing of over half the banks in the United States
   (3) the huge numbers of people seeking welfare relief
   (4) the lack of a strong and prepared American military
   (5) the stock market crash in the United States

8. Which of the following individuals was most likely the author of this passage?

   (1) a psychologist researching the effects of the Depression
   (2) an economist studying the causes of the Depression
   (3) someone who is very critical of today's Americans
   (4) one of the survivors of the 1929 Great Depression
   (5) someone who interviewed survivors of the Great Depression

9. Which of the following regions of the United States had already been suffering hardship?

   (1) the Great Lakes states
   (2) the Pacific coast
   (3) the Southwest
   (4) the Corn Belt
   (5) Appalachia

Questions 10–14 are based on the following passage.

There seemed to be no end to media attacks on Bill Clinton because of alleged womanizing while he was governor of Arkansas, during the presidential campaign—and even when he was in the White House. These attacks were just another chapter in the media's intrusion into a politician's personal life for the entertainment value it offers. The public's fascination with presidents' private lives is no recent phenomenon, however, and the media have long recognized that this prurient interest sells papers and increases ratings.

President Andrew Jackson was accused in his day of engaging in adultery when he wed his previously married wife before her divorce was actually final, a fact of which he was not aware.

President Grover Cleveland, who admitted to having fathered an illegitimate child before he ran for high office, was caricatured in the papers and taunted with the slogan "Ma, Ma, where's my Pa? Gone to the White House, ha, ha ha!"

President Warren Harding reputedly had an affair and fathered a child in a White House broom closet!

By and large, the American people want most of all to be entertained—not informed of the facts. One need only consider the sales figures for popular magazines such as *People* and tabloids such as the *National Star* and *National Enquirer* to be aware of this fact.

10. Which of the following does the author of this passage believe?

   (1) The media should not intrude into politicians' personal lives.
   (2) The public should not support certain politicians.
   (3) The public supported Bill Clinton despite his womanizing.
   (4) Bill Clinton should have been impeached because of his womanizing.
   (5) Only "squeaky-clean" candidates should be president.

11. Which of the following assumptions does the author make?

   (1) The behavior of politicians is of no interest to the American public.
   (2) The media are not concerned about reporting the facts as they find them.
   (3) The American public is willing to forgive politicians who make mistakes.
   (4) The focus on the behavior of presidents is a new development.
   (5) The media are the natural enemy of imperfect politicians.

12. Which of the following opinions does the author convey?

   (1) American voters are uninformed and uninterested.
   (2) Everyone has something to hide, especially politicians.
   (3) The media are exercising their authority properly.
   (4) Wrongdoing by presidents will not be tolerated by the public.
   (5) The media are giving the public precisely what it wants.

13. Many people argue that mistakes made by a private citizen before he or she seeks office should not be held to the same standard of scrutiny as those made by a candidate or a politician while in office. Which of the following would these people say is an unfair comparison in this editorial?

    (1) Clinton's behavior as a candidate and his behavior as president
    (2) Clinton's behavior as president and Cleveland's behavior as a private citizen
    (3) Clinton's behavior as a candidate and Cleveland's behavior as president
    (4) Cleveland's behavior as president and Harding's behavior as president
    (5) Jackson's behavior as president and Jackson's behavior as a candidate

14. Which of the following is *not* an idea supported by facts in this editorial?

    (1) People like to hear gossip about people in the public eye, including prominent politicians.
    (2) Mistakes made by presidents in their personal lives are not a new development.
    (3) The office of president of the United States demands the highest standards of conduct.
    (4) The media are just as guilty of engaging in sensationalism as the public is of demanding it.
    (5) Scandal is a tried-and-true method of selling papers and increasing ratings.

Questions 15 and 16 are based on the following excerpt.

Although some accommodations are being made to changing family structures, the bottom line of the message remains clear to anyone who has lived through it—the normal mother, the caring mother, the *good* mother, is at home. Ask any working parent who's tried to find a pediatrician at 7:00 A.M. or 9:00 P.M. Ask anyone who's tried to make special arrangements for appliance servicing or child care on school vacation days. Ask a parent who's tried to find adequate day care for an infant or preschooler. Many people believe that times have changed in the past few years and that women's (and men's) roles are different and more flexible. But as far as substantive, *real* changes in provisions for families with working mothers are concerned, there has been little more than rhetoric. Ask any working mother. Or father for that matter.

—Excerpted from *Mothers Who Work: Strategies for Coping* by Jeanne Bodin and Bonnie Mitelman

15. What is the main point of this excerpt?

    (1) Pediatricians should be more accommodating to working parents.
    (2) Mothers of young children should not work outside the home.
    (3) Society has not changed to provide for new family situations.
    (4) Children have suffered from changing non-traditional family structures.
    (5) Fathers should take on more domestic responsibilities.

16. What inference about the larger society's view of working mothers does this excerpt support?

    (1) They neglect and don't love their children.
    (2) They value their jobs over their children's welfare.
    (3) They are responsible for increased juvenile delinquency.
    (4) They are still treated unfairly by society.
    (5) They fall short in those areas that define a good mother.

Questions 17–20 are based on the following chart.

ECONOMIC INDICATORS										
	1929	**1933**	**1937**	**1939**	**1940**	**1941**	**1942**	**1943**	**1944**	**1945**
Gross National Product (GNP)	103.4	55.8	90.7	90.8	99.9	124.9	158.3	192.0	210.5	212.3
Personal Income	84.9	46.9	73.8	72.4	77.8	95.3	122.4	150.7	164.4	169.8
Consumer Price Index (CPI) 1967=100	51.3	38.8	43.0	41.6	42.0	44.1	48.8	51.8	52.7	53.9
Unemployment (in percent)	3.2	24.9	14.3	17.2	14.6	9.9	4.7	1.9	1.2	1.9

17. Economic indicators are statistics that show economic experts how the economy is performing. These can include the gross national product (GNP), the level of personal income, the consumer price index (CPI), and the unemployment rate in the country. According to the chart, which one of the years listed showed the most severe effects of the Great Depression?

(1) 1929
(2) 1933
(3) 1937
(4) 1939
(5) 1940

18. In 1941 the United States entered World War II. By 1945 the war was nearing an end. According to the statistics in the chart, what was the effect of America's involvement in the war on the economy?

(1) It weakened the economy.
(2) It made the economy healthier.
(3) It led to a decrease in the GNP.
(4) It led to a decrease in the CPI.
(5) It had no measurable effect on the economy.

19. Which of the following factors would best account for low unemployment during the period from 1941 to 1945?

(1) Public work projects such as the CCC (Civilian Conservation Corps) created jobs.
(2) Factories were at peak production levels as they contributed to the war effort.
(3) The government created many jobs for the unemployed.
(4) Children joined their mothers on the production lines, increasing the number of workers.
(5) Relatively few jobs left the country because the foreign labor pool was limited.

20. According to the chart, the prices of the 1930s and early 1940s were closest to which of the following?

(1) the prices in 1967
(2) half the level of prices in 1967
(3) double the level of prices in 1967
(4) the prices in 2001
(5) half the level of prices in 2001

Questions 21–23 are based on the following passage.

Until Levittown, suburbia was only for the rich and the upper middle class. But Levittown was different. All of its houses were built from the same floor plans; there was no center of town, no industry, no history. Its houses were built explicitly for World War II veterans, and they were affordably priced. They cost $6,990 in 1947, and for this the returning servicemen got a two-bedroom Cape Cod or ranch-style house on a 60-by-100 foot lot and a federally subsidized mortgage of $65 a month. Today the basic, unremodeled version sells for over $125,000 with property taxes of $3,000 to $4,000 a year.

21. What does the passage suggest about the first residents of Levittown?

They were
(1) wealthy
(2) upper middle class
(3) middle class
(4) poverty stricken
(5) of all classes

22. Levittown in 1947 was a highly regulated community. Only carousel-style clotheslines were permitted, lawns had to be mowed once a week (or owners were billed for the service), and no African Americans were allowed to own or rent houses there. If a community were to set such rules today, they could be punished for violating which of the following?

(1) the First Amendment of the U.S. Constitution, which guarantees free speech and freedom of assembly
(2) the 1968 Federal Housing Act, which forbade racial discrimination in federally financed housing
(3) the 1964 Civil Rights Act, which outlawed racial discrimination in public accommodation and hiring practices
(4) the 1954 Supreme Court decision that racial segregation in public schools is unconstitutional
(5) the 1896 Supreme Court decision that approved separate but equal facilities for all races

23. The passage cites major drawbacks to living in many suburbs. Which is a disadvantage that is not cited?

(1) great distance from the city
(2) no main commercial core
(3) no interesting background
(4) no industrial tax base
(5) fast-rising costs of houses

Questions 24–25 are based on the following passage.

The city of Chicago that was destroyed by the kick of a kerosene lantern on October 8, 1871, was a hustling, bustling hub of industry and transportation, but it was not glamorous. It was dirty and had many unpaved streets and crude wooden structures. After the fire, Chicagoans were determined to reconstruct a more attractive mecca for the immigrants who flocked to it. Laborers of every trade moved to the midwestern city to help in the tremendous task of rebuilding. But in 1873, financial panic and a drop in construction forced huge numbers of workers out of their jobs. Anger and frustration soon developed into riots and bloodshed. Unionism in Chicago was off to a stormy start.

24. According to this passage, why did unions start in Chicago?

(1) because working conditions were bad
(2) because so many people were losing their jobs
(3) because there was too much violence in the city
(4) because the city had been destroyed by fire
(5) because it was no longer an industrial center

25. Which of the following opinions about Chicago before the fire can be found in this excerpt?

(1) It was an important center for industry.
(2) Many railroads led into and out of it.
(3) It was exciting but unglamorous.
(4) It had many unpaved streets.
(5) The buildings there were mostly wooden.

Questions 26 and 27 are based on the following map.

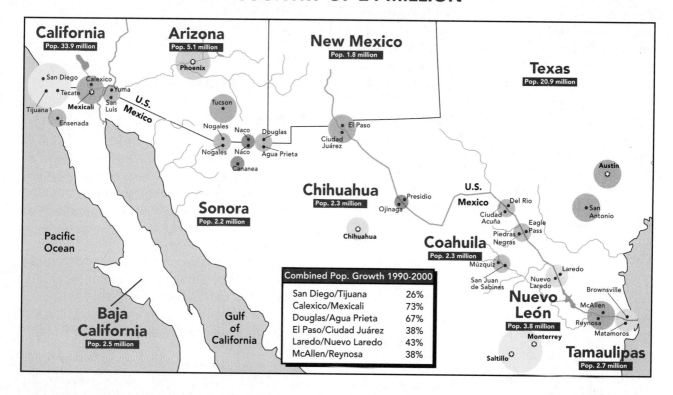

A COUNTRY OF 24 MILLION

Combined Pop. Growth 1990-2000	
San Diego/Tijuana	26%
Calexico/Mexicali	73%
Douglas/Agua Prieta	67%
El Paso/Ciudad Juárez	38%
Laredo/Nuevo Laredo	43%
McAllen/Reynosa	38%

26. Which of the following hypotheses is best supported by the information on this map?

(1) The NAFTA agreement, which reduced U.S.-Mexican trade barriers, has been a stimulant to growth on the border.

(2) The drug war has made the border a very dangerous and inhospitable place to live and work.

(3) By effectively reducing illegal immigration, the Immigration and Naturalization Service (INS) has encouraged growth.

(4) U.S. citizens have been moving to the border region because of its superior quality of life.

(5) Because they have been developed and expanded too rapidly, the border communities are a disaster waiting to happen.

27. The 2000 Census found that McAllen and Laredo are two of the ten fastest growing Metropolitan areas in the United States. This information, along with the map, best supports which of the following predictions?

(1) In order to protect American jobs, the United States will reestablish tariffs on goods manufactured in Mexico.

(2) The border region will become the most desirable area of the United States in which to live.

(3) The abundance of jobs in the border region will make improving educational skills a low priority for workers.

(4) The economy of the border region is in danger of overheating, triggering inflation.

(5) The population of the border region will continue to increase rapidly in the next decade.

Questions 28 and 29 are based on the following passage.

In the eyes of Washington, Senator Jim Jeffords took on a whole new identity last week. Switching parties is a big deal here, akin to a sex-change operation. But in Vermont, the Jeffords of this week seems little different from last week's—independent, pro-tree, pro-choice, pro-special ed. In the eyes of the country, it's George Bush's identity—consummate professional, protean charmer, reasonable conservative—that has become mottled. Bush campaigned as an adult who would restore not only honor but also professionalism to the White House. No all-night sessions strewn with pizza boxes. He would institute appropriate dress, muted cell phones and meetings that started—and ended—on time.

So how did this smooth Bush operation lose Jeffords? First, by its simple failure to recognize that Bush needed him more than he needed Bush. Grownups know that little things matter (Newt Gingrich shut down the government when he didn't like his seat on Air Force One) and that relationships are based on respect and reciprocity. Enamored of the corporate model, the Bushies treated Jeffords like some fungible account executive who could be replaced at will instead of recognizing that in a fifty-fifty Senate, every Senator is king. White House staff rarely saved Jeffords a seat at the table, and even tried to end-run him on the committee he chaired. He wasn't invited to a routine Rose Garden ceremony for a Vermonter named Teacher of the Year, and was reportedly denied his ration of West Wing tour passes. If it was just an oversight (their explanation), they hardly look like management geniuses. If it was a ham-handed snub (everyone else's explanation), it showed how petty they could be.

In six months, Democrats hadn't been able to define Bush as bent on satisfying his right wing at the cost of the center. Jeffords did that in one press conference. The debate shifted overnight to whether Bush could continue to govern from the right. Already, moderates are getting attention: John McCain was invited for dinner, Olympia Snowe got her calls returned, Arlen Specter got a leadership post.

—Excerpted from "The Centrist Doesn't Hold" by Margaret Carlson, *Time Magazine*, June 4, 2001

28. When Jim Jeffords switched his affiliation from Republican to Independent in June 2001, it was the first time in American history that control of one of the houses of Congress had shifted between elections. What does the author think was the crucial factor in that switch?

    (1) the failure of the Democrats to define Bush as "right wing"
    (2) the differences between Bush and Jeffords on the issues
    (3) Bush's professional, businesslike approach to government
    (4) the arrogance and immaturity of the White House staff
    (5) the increasingly conservative views of the Republicans

29. How was Jeffords able, in one press conference, to define President George W. Bush as "bent on satisfying his right wing at the cost of the center"?

    (1) He delivered an eloquent speech outlining Bush's shortcomings.
    (2) He decided against accepting a position in the Republican leadership.
    (3) He showed how independent and strong-willed Vermonters could be.
    (4) He announced that he was leaving the Republican Party.
    (5) He denounced his poor treatment at the hands of the White House.

Questions 30–32 are based on the following passage.

Few occurrences in recent history have been as stunning as the breakup of the Soviet dictatorship at the turn of the 1990s. Few have raised as many gleaming hopes for bettering the human condition. And few seem to have had their promise so quickly dashed in actuality.

It is all too easy to forget from the vantage point of the late 1990s that when Mikhail Gorbachev's reign yielded to Yeltsin's in 1990–1991 we had good reason to think that we were witnessing a transition of regimes. Not only did the Communist Party of the Soviet Union relinquish its hold on power after more than 70 years. In quitting the scene, it appeared to discredit the socialist model of economic and social organization and, indeed, to pull down in its wake the U.S.S.R. itself as a multinational state, a regional hegemon lording it over Eastern Europe, and a global superpower. The successor states to the U.S.S.R.—the rump Russian Federation and 14 smaller independent countries—seemed to many in the West to be destined to reinvent themselves as law-abiding members of the international community, internally democratic and prepared to seek prosperity through market economics. The Clinton administration took precisely that official line: over and over, it reassured us that Russia and the rest were "building" democracy and markets—gamely carpentering away despite a few rough spots here and there—and were constructing a cooperative strategic relationship with the United States. Given Russia's size, huge arsenal of weapons of mass destruction, and mineral and petroleum riches, such an image was reassuring to Western policy makers.

No one . . . buys this rosy image any longer. It is in the economic and socioeconomic realm that the signs of crisis are most alarming. Although the liberalization of state controls over economic activity, the privatization of many assets, and the opening up of Russia to the global economy did bring some benefits after 1991—the disappearance for the time being of queues at shops and the free availability of consumer goods in particular—the brave talk of achieving economic efficiency and prosperity within a few months or years has been cruelly disappointed. National output, having contracted every year this decade except 1997, dropped about 7 percent in 1998. The nascent business class, many of its profits conveniently deposited in foreign bank accounts, has shunned investment in domestic economic development and has for the most part displayed no sense of civic conscience or fellow feeling for ordinary people. Social services, the civil bureaucracy, and the armed forces have been starved of resources, but otherwise not reformed or improved. The state's inability to collect more than a fraction of the taxes owing gives it an inbuilt budget deficit and thereby exerts constant pressure on the currency.

So mismanaged was Russia's economic reform, whose fizzling is at the heart of the present debacle, that it was only a matter of time before its contradictions caught up with it. Insider privatization, overregulation, punitive and arbitrary taxation, an inconsistent legal framework, and lackadaisical prosecution of criminals and gangsters prompted the beneficiaries of the first waves of reform to shelter their winnings offshore and scared away most foreign investors. Three-quarters of all transactions in the industrial economy are conducted in barter, bypassing money and taxes.

Wages, pensions, and social allowances arrive months in arrears for tens of millions of Russians. Barely bothering to explain to the mass public the reasons for change or its unpalatable consequences, politicians have found ingenious ways to keep insolvent firms afloat and to delay the restructuring of industry.

—Excerpted from "Russia Stalled," *Harvard* Magazine, March–April 1999

30. What is the overall picture of Russia painted by this article?

  (1) a formerly great nation struggling to come back
  (2) a nation preyed upon by greedy neighbors
  (3) a politically and economically dysfunctional nation
  (4) a powerful, threatening superpower
  (5) a thriving, prosperous, well-managed nation

31. All but which of the following are reasons for Russia's current problems?

  (1) the breakup of the Soviet dictatorship
  (2) insider privatization of state-owned businesses
  (3) chaotic and arbitrary taxation system
  (4) lack of domestic and foreign investment
  (5) the reduction of resources for public services

32. What action might have the greatest effect in improving the situation in Russia?

  (1) the Russian military's dismantling its huge nuclear arsenal
  (2) political leaders' reducing corruption in the government
  (3) foreign nations' increasing financial and humanitarian aid
  (4) foreign investors' increasing their investment in new businesses
  (5) reducing the rate of privatization of state-owned companies

Questions 33 and 34 are based on the following passage.

"When you look around the country for visual evidence of African-American history and existence, you find very few institutions where this history is preserved," says Henry N. Tisdale, the president of Clafin College in Orangeburg, S.C. "I'm thinking, of course, of the black church as one, but the other is our colleges and universities. Many of our high schools and the like have been bulldozed. The only places where you find archives and great collections of our artifacts and our history are on these campuses of the historically black colleges and universities. We have the buildings, we have the artifacts, we have the books."

—Excerpted from "African-American Colleges," *Preservation*, March/April 1999

33. Which of the following would Henry N. Tisdale probably think was most important?

  (1) preserving historical artifacts and books on historically African American campuses
  (2) preserving and restoring historically African American churches
  (3) expanding affirmative action programs in all colleges and universities
  (4) building replicas of destroyed historically African American high schools
  (5) integrating all historically African American colleges and universities

34. The role that historically black colleges and universities play in the African American community is most similar to which of the following?

  (1) women's colleges for the women's movement
  (2) synagogues in the Jewish community
  (3) art museums in major cities
  (4) shopping malls in suburban communities
  (5) ancient burial grounds for Native Americans

Questions 35 and 36 are based on the following map.

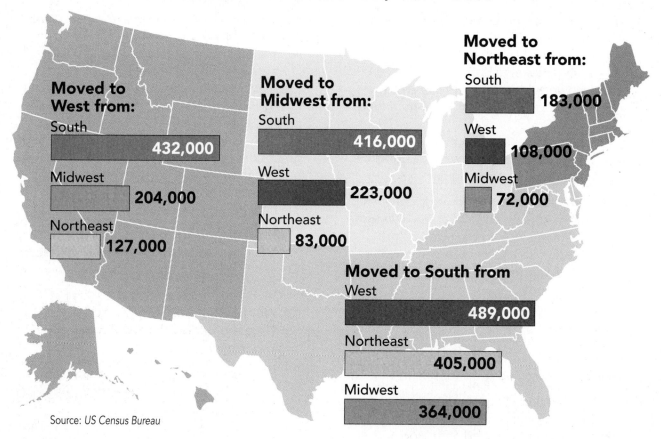

WHERE PEOPLE MOVED, 1999–2000

Moved to West from:
South
432,000

Midwest
204,000

Northeast
127,000

Moved to Midwest from:
South
416,000

West
223,000

Northeast
83,000

Moved to Northeast from:
South
183,000

West
108,000

Midwest
72,000

Moved to South from
West
489,000

Northeast
405,000

Midwest
364,000

Source: US Census Bureau

35. Many Americans moved from one region of the country to another during the 1990s. Which two regions of the United States had the greatest imbalance in Americans moving from one region to the other?

(1) the South and the West
(2) the Northeast and the Midwest
(3) the West and the Midwest
(4) the South and the Northeast
(5) the South and the Midwest

36. Which of the following is the most likely reason why the greatest number of people moved to the South between 1999–2000?

(1) There is a booming technology sector in the South.
(2) The weather in the South is warmer than in other parts of the country.
(3) The South is known for its hospitality and beautiful countryside.
(4) There are more jobs available in the South than in other parts of the country.
(5) The biggest cities in the United States are located in the South.

Questions 37 and 38 are based on the following chart.

PERCENTAGE CHANGE FROM PREVIOUS YEAR FOR U.S. CRIMES						
Year	Violent crime	Murder	Rape	Assault	Burglary	Theft	Auto Theft
1996	−6.5%	−9.1%	−1.7%	−6.3%	−3.6%	−1.3%	−5.2%
1997	−3.2%	−7.3%	−0.1%	−1.4%	−1.8%	−2.3%	−2.9%
1998	−6.4%	−7.1%	−3.2%	−4.8%	−5.3%	−4.8%	−8.4%
1999	−6.7%	−8.5%	−4.3%	−6.2%	−10.0%	−5.7%	−7.7%
2000	0.1%	−1.1%	0.7%	0.4%	−2.1%	0.1%	2.7%

Source: *FBI*

37. From 1996 to 2000, which crime decreased the most on average?

   (1) murder
   (2) rape
   (3) assault
   (4) burglary
   (5) auto theft

38. Which of the following best describes the trend in violent crimes from 1996 to 2000?

   (1) Violent crime decreased throughout the entire period.
   (2) After increasing, violent crime began to decrease in 2000.
   (3) Violent crime increased throughout the entire period.
   (4) Violent crime fluctuated from year to year.
   (5) After decreasing, violent crime slightly increased in 2000.

Questions 39 and 40 are based on the following graph and maps.

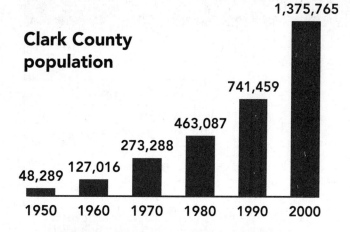

Clark County population

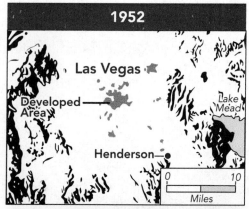

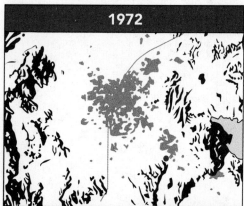

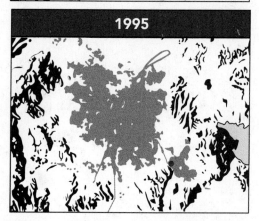

39. Which prediction is best supported by the graph and the maps?

(1) Growth in Las Vegas has already peaked and will dramatically slow down.

(2) After growing too fast, Las Vegas will face an economic downturn in the next decade.

(3) Growth and development in Las Vegas will probably continue in the near future.

(4) Las Vegas will probably adopt strict controls on sprawl and new development soon.

(5) Las Vegas will eventually become the largest city in the Western United States.

40. What will be the greatest challenge to continued growth and prosperity in Las Vegas?

(1) building enough new schools and hospitals

(2) building enough roads to avoid gridlock

(3) finding more room for expansion

(4) developing enough sources of energy

(5) finding sufficient supplies of water

Questions 41and 42 are based on the following passage.

"The United States will be the first to usher in a socialist republic," predicted August Bebel, the leader of the German Social Democratic party, in 1907. A contemporary, Karl Kautsky, the German's party's leading theoretician, was equally sanguine: class conflict, he believed, was "overdue" in America, and developing "more sharply" there than anywhere else in the world.

Bebel, Kautsky, and other European observers based their judgments in part on the growing power of the American Socialist party during the early years of the 20th century. In 1912, candidates on the party's slate were elected to municipal offices across the country, and its leader, Eugene V. Debs, running for the the presidency, received fully 6 percent of the national vote.

But 1912 also proved to be a high-water mark. A brief eight years later, the party lay in ruins, its leader Debs serving a prison term for agitation against World War I, its ties to the trade-union movement and the electorate sundered. While, in the decades to come, social-democratic and labor parties were to emerge as powerful electoral forces throughout Europe and the English-speaking world, no radical left-wing party was ever to achieve such a foothold in the United States.

—Excerpted from "Left Out, It Didn't Happen Here: Why Socialism Failed in the United States," *Commentary*, October 2000

41. Of the following, which was the least likely to contribute to the demise of the American Socialist Party?

(1) the absence of rigid class distinctions in the United States
(2) the highly individualistic ethos of the American people
(3) its opposition to American participation in World War I
(4) its public position of opposition to organized religion
(5) its support of a national system of unemployment insurance

42. Which American political development would least surprise Bebel and Kautsky?

(1) Roosevelt's New Deal, which implemented much of the Socialist agenda
(2) the victory of Reagan and supply-side economics in the 1980s
(3) the triumph of capitalism over socialism in the late twentieth century
(4) the strength of the anticommunist movement during the 1950s
(5) the decline of the American Socialist Party in the 1920s and 1930s

 Go to **www.GEDSocialStudies.com** for additional practice and instruction!

Question 43 is based on the following political cartoon.

43. This cartoon is based on the painting American Gothic, which shows a typical American farming couple. What is the cartoonist trying to convey to his audience?

    (1) Immigration is destroying the American way of life.
    (2) Typical Americans can be of Asian and African as well as European descent.
    (3) Multiracial couples are taking over American family farms.
    (4) Minority Americans are forgetting their original cultures.
    (5) Americans should be encouraged to live and work on farms.

Questions 44 and 45 are based on the following photograph and caption.

During an atomic bomb test, a cloud rises from the desert floor, seven miles from observers in the foreground at Yucca Flat, Nevada.

44. From this photograph, which of the following conclusions can be drawn?

    (1) Important scientific data was gathered by observing an atomic bomb test.
    (2) The observers were far enough away from the test to be safe.
    (3) The observers were unaware of the harmful effects of radiation.
    (4) The military needed to show that it possessed atomic bombs.
    (5) An atomic-bomb blast is a beautiful and exciting spectacle.

45. For what reason might the United States government have encouraged the taking and publishing of this photograph?

    (1) to show how beautiful an atomic-bomb blast could be
    (2) to promote taking precautions when working with radiation
    (3) to encourage those working for a ban on atomic-bomb testing
    (4) to maintain popular support for the atomic-bomb testing program
    (5) to help those present to qualify for federal payments for radiation related illness

Questions 46 and 47 are based on the following passage.

Think of all the dreams that were shattered, careers that were ruined and money that was lost as a result of the birth of the huge industries that developed around oil, telephones, movies, automobiles, airplanes, semiconductors and personal computers. Working with young companies can be dangerous for anyone. It doesn't matter whether that was in Akron, Ohio, in the 1870s, Detroit in the 1920s or Santa Clara, California, in the 1990s.

In Silicon Valley the cycle of enthusiasm and disappointment has been compressed as the years have gone by and the pace of innovation has increased. The 1960s spawned the rise of the semi-conductor business. The 1970s brought personal computers. The 1980s gave us computer-networking companies and biotech firms. And the 1990s produced a rush of Internet companies. Each of these waves was followed by disappointments as hundreds of weak companies collapsed or were gobbled up by their larger competitors. But all these periods gave rise to the formation of a handful of venture capital-backed firms that have come to occupy major roles the U.S. and the global economy, such as Intel, Compaq, Amgen, Microsoft, Sun Microsystems, Dell, AOL, Oracle and Cisco Systems.

—Excerpted from "Spring Comes Early to Silicon Valley" by Michael Moritz, *Time Magazine*, March 26, 2001

46. What is the main point that the author is trying to make?

   (1) The current situation in Silicon Valley is a new phenomenon.
   (2) The next decade will see the growth of another new industry.
   (3) It is always better to work in an established company.
   (4) Silicon Valley is the current heartland of American innovation.
   (5) The growth of new industries usually follows a similar pattern.

47. Which of the following is a reasonable conclusion based on the information in the passage?

   (1) Some major Internet companies will survive the current downturn.
   (2) Amazon.com will come to occupy a major role in the U.S. economy.
   (3) Powerful companies such as Microsoft will force out newcomers.
   (4) Young companies have a poor record of worker safety.
   (5) The next area of rapid growth will be based in electronics.

Question 48 is based on the following painting.

48. What is the value most promoted by this painting, The Spirit of '76, by Archibald Willard?

   (1) the futility of solving problems through violence
   (2) the importance of music in all aspects of life
   (3) the nobility of participating in American triumphs
   (4) the need for different generations to work together
   (5) performing well even under adverse conditions

Questions 49 and 50 are based on the following picture and passage.

This view of Birmingham, a major industrial city in the English Midlands, dates from 1886. In the background is the vast industrial section of the city. Dozens of factories are spewing smoke into the atmosphere.

In the foreground is the main square of Birmingham. It is surrounded by beautiful public buildings, including a museum, an art gallery, a library, and the town hall. Between the elegant town square and the gritty industrial area is the glass roof of the railroad station. The public buildings were built to last, and remained in the city long after its days as one of the world's centers of heavy industry had passed.

49. What is the main idea expressed by both the picture and the passage?

(1) Birmingham was a hideous, polluted eyesore.
(2) There was both ugliness and beauty in Birmingham.
(3) The only way to afford grand public buildings is through industry.
(4) The beautiful buildings outlasted the ugly factories.
(5) The train station was the heart of Birmingham.

50. The builders of Birmingham's public buildings were probably unaware of which of the following?

(1) The money to build was provided by the city's industry.
(2) There was limited green space in the city.
(3) These buildings might last more than a century.
(4) Air pollution could be damaging to the buildings.
(5) The workers in the factories led difficult lives.

Answers are on pages 133–135.

Chapter 2

Places and People

GED Social Studies pages 157–181
Complete GED pages 427–443

Questions 1–4 are based on the following passage.

The ring of axes and the crash of falling trees echoed up and down the coasts of the land which the white man now called New England. Settlements began crowding in upon each other. In 1625 some of the colonists asked Samoset to give them twelve thousand additional acres of Pemaquid land. Samoset knew that land came from the Great Spirit, was as endless as the sky, and belonged to no one. To humor these strangers in their strange ways, however, he went through a ceremony of transferring the land and made his mark on a paper for them. It was the first deed of Indian land to English colonists.

—Excerpted from *Bury My Heart at Wounded Knee* by Dee Brown.

1. Who was Samoset?

   (1) a British colonist
   (2) an American builder
   (3) a European trader
   (4) a Native American leader
   (5) a religious fanatic

2. The purchase by the Dutch of Manhattan Island from local natives for $24 worth of kettles and beads, together with Samoset's deeding of the Pemaquid land to settlers for a nominal sum, supports which of the following conclusions about Native Americans?

   (1) They did not know and appreciate the true value of land.
   (2) They were tricked into selling their land for so little.
   (3) They viewed property ownership differently from Europeans.
   (4) They prized shiny trinkets and utensils more than they prized land.
   (5) They were generous people who wanted to help the newcomers.

3. The purchase of Manhattan Island by the Dutch and Samoset's deeding of the Pemaquid land for a nominal sum demonstrate which of the following American beliefs?

   (1) Money is the root of all evil.
   (2) Money can buy anything.
   (3) Money cannot buy happiness.
   (4) Money does not grow on trees.
   (5) Money makes money.

4. Which of the following statements contains a faulty conclusion?

   (1) If land belongs to no one, no one can deed it.
   (2) If the Great Spirit provides land, it is as endless as the sky.
   (3) If land belongs to no one, it cannot belong to the Pemaquid.
   (4) If the Great Spirit provides land, it really belongs to Him alone.
   (5) If the Europeans asked for deeds, they believed the Pemaquid really owned the land.

Questions 5–8 are based on the map below.

ACTIVE MEDICAL DOCTORS PER 100,000 POPULATION IN 1990

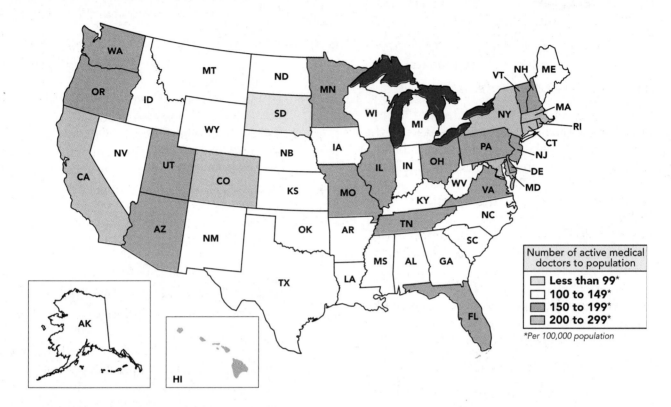

5. According to the map, what was the ratio of doctors to people in Alaska in 1990?

(1) 100–149 per 100,000 people
(2) 150–199 per 100,000 people
(3) 200–249 per 100,000 people
(4) 250–299 per 100,000 people
(5) over 300 per 100,000 people

6. What characteristics do states with the greatest number of doctors per population tend to have?

(1) southeastern, urban, industrial
(2) southeastern, rural, agricultural
(3) midwestern, urban, industrial
(4) northeastern, urban, industrial
(5) western, urban, industrial

7. Which of the following statements can you infer from the map?

(1) The need for doctors in Idaho and Wyoming was less in 1990 than the need in New York, Massachusetts, and Connecticut.
(2) There is a direct connection between how many people live in a state and the number of active doctors it has.
(3) Residents of Oklahoma, Arkansas, and Mississippi suffered from chronic health problems in the 1990s because there weren't enough doctors.
(4) The high density of doctors in the Northeast may be connected to the large number of medical schools and hospitals in those states.
(5) In 1990 the majority of states had 151–200 doctors per 100,000 people, which was more than were needed.

8. One southeastern state with a fairly high number of doctors per 100,000 people is Florida. Which of the following factors would *not* contribute to Florida's higher ratio of doctors to people?

   (1) It is more urban than its neighbors.
   (2) It has a better climate than its neighbors.
   (3) It is home to a growing number of industries.
   (4) Many well-to-do elderly people have moved there.
   (5) It has become the most populous southeastern state.

Questions 9 and 10 are based on the following passage.

The Pacific man does not see the ocean as implacable and hostile. He is incapable of weeping on the beach as do Portuguese fisher folk when their boats put out. He has none of the dread of the sea that is found in the bittersweet regard of the Scotch and the New Englanders. The Pacific man sees the ocean as Olympian . . . outsized and majestic, capable of enormous power, but also capable of foolishness and mistakes. It gives his life all the tension it needs.

There is, I think, a reason for this. Throughout Oceania, in the great archipelagoes with their vast sweeps of salt water and their tiny specks of islands, men have not yet dominated nature. Nature is lived with gingerly, delicately, sometimes with zest and daring, but always with awe and sometimes with a crawling eerie fear. Not having mastered nature, the man of Oceania has little desire to master other men. His art, his politics, his manners, his religion, his industry all seem miniature and bleached and diminished because of a looming presence: the Pacific.

—Excerpted from *The Blue of Capricorn* by Eugene Burdick. Copyright © 1961 by Eugene Burdick, renewed 1989. Reprinted by permission of Houghton Mifflin Company. All rights reserved.

9. Which of the following theories is supported by the passage above?

   (1) Development of a culture is affected by the natural environment in which it grows.
   (2) Primitive civilizations have developed better control over nature than more advanced ones.
   (3) Populations that depend on the sea for livelihood are less sophisticated culturally than those that do not.
   (4) The structure of a society is determined by the race and cultural characteristics of its inhabitants.
   (5) The people of a region are as dangerous to other people as nature has been to them.

10. What can you conclude about Pacific Islanders, given the information in the passage?

    Pacific Islanders
    (1) are not willing to become westernized
    (2) have developed complicated music and dances
    (3) have accepted Christianity as their religion
    (4) are less restrained than Europeans
    (5) seldom become involved in wars

Questions 11 and 12 refer to the following cartoon.

Questions 13 and 14 are based on the following diagram

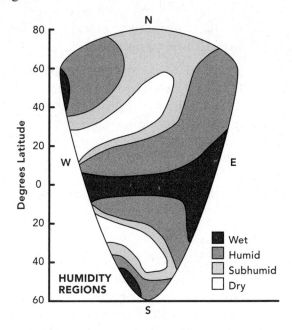

11. From this cartoon, what can you infer about the cartoonist?

The cartoonist
(1) approves of the President's plan to involve big energy companies in forming his energy policy
(2) agrees that big energy companies, like oil, coal, and nuclear energy, are good for the economy
(3) is annoyed at the fuss that environmentalists are making about the President's energy policy
(4) is pleased that the President has established a tradition of playing sports like T-ball at the White House
(5) is concerned that the President's preference for big business will have a negative impact on the earth

12. If there were a fourth player on the T-ball team, which of the following would it be?

(1) gas
(2) solar
(3) steel
(4) thermal
(5) auto

13. This diagram of a hypothetical continent shows a general pattern of predicted humidity. According to the diagram, where is the largest area of high humidity?

(1) the northernmost point of the continent
(2) the southernmost point of the continent
(3) about 20 degrees north of the equator
(4) about 20 degrees south of the equator
(5) the equatorial region of the continent

14. In general, how does the humidity of the west coast compare to the east coast?

The west coast tends to be
(1) more humid than the east coast
(2) less humid than the east coast
(3) as humid as the east coast
(4) more humid in its northern region than its southern region
(5) less humid in its northern region than in its southern region

Questions 15–17 are based on the following passage.

The German Jews who fled from Hitler were different from the ghetto and eastern European Jews. They were not devout Zionists but had largely been assimilated into German society. They were not pioneers and merchants; they were doctors and lawyers and scientists and artisans.

15. This passage implies which of the following about ghetto and eastern European Jews?

    They were not usually
    (1) staunchly religious
    (2) professional workers
    (3) adventurous pioneers
    (4) ambitious merchants
    (5) urban residents

16. What does the writer of this passage assume?

    (1) Devout Zionists did not easily assimilate into cultures around them.
    (2) German Jews were less ambitious than their other European counterparts.
    (3) European Jews were seldom able to handle full-time jobs.
    (4) Zionists did not have as many educational opportunities as German Jews.
    (5) German Jews deserved more respect than other European Jews.

17. From this passage, what can we infer that *ghetto* means?

    (1) a place where people speak slang
    (2) a place with distinct architecture
    (3) an ancient religious group
    (4) a nonintegrated community
    (5) northern European

Questions 18–21 are based on the following descriptions of types of maps.

Topographical—a map that shows geographical land features of an area

Population—a map that explains the distribution of people within an area

World—a map that depicts the entire world in order to compare facts from all over the globe

Weather—a map that describes current or forecasted weather and climate

Political—a map that outlines borders between countries, states, or territories, shows trade relationships between countries, and indicates systems of government

18. Which kind of map would depict the movements of the Allied armies in Europe during World War I?

    (1) a topographical map
    (2) a population map
    (3) a world map
    (4) a weather map
    (5) a political map

19. Which kind of map would best show the number of minority-group members in the city and suburbs of a metropolis?

    (1) a topographical map
    (2) a population map
    (3) a world map
    (4) a weather map
    (5) a political map

20. What kind of map would show the average annual snowfall in a region?

    (1) a topographical map
    (2) a population map
    (3) a world map
    (4) a weather map
    (5) a political map

21. As part of military training, army recruits are required to pass a test on orienteering. In orienteering the soldier is given a time limit in which to cover unfamiliar territory by using a map and a compass. What type of map would be most useful in this task?

    (1) a topographical map
    (2) a population map
    (3) a world map
    (4) a weather map
    (5) a political map

Questions 22–24 are based on the map below.

Land Use

▦	Tundra
▨	Grassland
□	Mid-Latitude Forest
▩	Tropical Forest
▬	Cultivated Land
▧	Barren Land

22. Which of the following statements is adequately supported by information on the map?

    (1) Several different types of crops can be grown in Alaska.
    (2) Canada has much fertile farmland.
    (3) Central America has almost no tillable land.
    (4) The western United States has relatively little cropland.
    (5) Mexico is plagued with great expanses of barren land.

23. Where is tundra land found?

    In the
    (1) far northern frigid areas
    (2) western mountain ranges
    (3) central plains
    (4) warm southern regions
    (5) eastern coastlines

24. In which of the following regions are lumber industries most likely to prosper?

    (1) northern Canada
    (2) the Midwestern United States
    (3) central Mexico
    (4) the Eastern seaboard of the United States
    (5) Alaska's northwest

Questions 25 and 26 are based on the following chart.

OCCUPATIONAL DISTRIBUTION OF CHICANOS, 1930
by States of the Southwest and Sex (percentages)

Occupational Level	Texas		New Mexico		Colorado		Arizona		California		Southwest	
	M	F	M	F	M	F	M	F	M	F	M	F
Professional and Technical	0.8	2.9	0.5	3.6	0.3	1.0	0.6	3.4	1.0	3.0	0.9	2.9
Managers, Proprietors, and Officials	3.4	2.6	1.3	2.8	0.4	0.4	2.9	3.3	1.9	1.8	2.8	2.4
Clerical	1.1	4.3	0.5	3.6	0.3	2.1	1.4	8.2	1.0	9.5	1.0	5.8
Sales	2.6	4.4	1.3	2.5	0.6	1.4	2.7	6.6	2.2	4.1	2.4	4.3
Craftsmen and Foremen (skilled)	7.3	0.4	4.6	0.3	2.2	0.3	7.9	0.5	7.0	1.4	6.8	0.6
Operatives (semiskilled)	6.1	16.4	19.2	9.0	14.7	6.3	26.1	13.1	8.1	40.8	9.1	21.9
Laborers (unskilled)	23.6	2.3	20.7	1.6	25.3	3.4	26.5	1.5	37.6	4.7	28.2	2.8
Service	4.2	39.7	3.0	67.2	1.7	41.6	3.0	55.0	4.2	27.5	4.0	38.4
Farm Laborers	35.0	25.9	35.1	5.2	48.8	41.5	26.4	7.9	35.7	7.1	35.1	19.7
Farmers and Farm Managers	15.9	1.2	13.9	4.2	5.7	2.1	2.5	0.6	1.3	0.1	9.8	1.0

25. What is the most likely reason that the chart focuses on states in the Southwest?

(1) The sociologists who collected the information live in the Southwest and prefer to work close to home.

(2) Because of its dry climate, the Southwest is the easiest part of the country in which to gather this kind of data.

(3) Information about Chicanos (Mexican Americans) had been gathered previously in the other regions but not in the Southwest.

(4) Most Mexican Americans move to the Southwest from northern states because of better job opportunities.

(5) The Southwest is the region closest to the Mexican border and therefore has the greatest concentration of Mexican Americans.

26. In which occupational area did the largest percentage of southwestern Mexican American women work in 1930?

(1) management
(2) sales
(3) unskilled labor
(4) service
(5) farm labor

Questions 27–30 refer to the following passage.

Twelve years ago, the soon-to-be infamous barge, the Khian Sea, left the territorial waters of the United States and began circling the oceans in search of a country willing to accept its cargo: 14,000 tons of toxic incinerator ash.

First it went to the Bahamas, then to the Dominican Republic, Honduras, Bermuda, Guinea Bissau and the Netherlands Antilles. Wherever it went, people gathered to protest its arrival. No one wanted the hundreds of thousands of pounds of Philadelphia ash dumped in their country. Desperate to unload, the ship's crew lied about their cargo, hoping to catch a government unawares. Sometimes they identified the ash as "construction material," other times they said it was road fill, and still others "muddy waste." But environmental experts were generally one step ahead in notifying the recipients; no one would take it. That is, until it got to Haiti. There, officials were told it was the "fertilizer" they'd ordered, and four thousand tons of the ash was dumped onto the beach in the town of Gonaïves.

It didn't take Haitian officials long to realize they weren't getting fertilizer. They canceled the import permit and ordered the waste returned to the ship. But the Khian Sea slipped away in the night, leaving the toxic ash on the beach.

For two more years the Khian Sea went from country to country, to no avail, trying to dispose of the remaining 10,000 tons. The crew even painted over the barge's name— not once, but twice. Still, no one was fooled into taking its toxic cargo. A crew member later testified that the waste was finally dumped, when no one was looking, into the Indian Ocean.

—Excerpted from "Toxic Wastes and The New World Order" by Mitchell Cohen, in Synthesis/Regeneration 23: A Magazine of Green Social Thought, Fall 2000

27. What do the countries where the Khian Sea attempted to dump their waste have in common?

(1) They are all colonies of European countries.
(2) They have all accepted toxic waste from the United States.
(3) They are all located in the Indian Ocean.
(4) They are all relatively poor countries.
(5) They all import fertilizer from the United States.

28. Which of the following is *least* likely to occur as a result of the dumping of the Khian Sea's cargo?

(1) The company that owns the boat will clean up the dumping sites in Haiti and the Indian Ocean.
(2) High rates of cancer and birth defects in newborns will be reported in and around Gonaïves.
(3) Greenpeace and other environmental groups will organize rallies to protest the dumping.
(4) Similar episodes of toxic dumping will be reported in poor, underdeveloped countries.
(5) Scientific researchers will continue to try to find ways of more safely disposing of waste.

29. The incident involving the Khian Sea is most similar to which of the following situations?

(1) A person with a cheap watch sells it at a profit by persuading someone else that it is of great value.
(2) A distant relative comes to visit, stays too long, and leaves your house in a shambles when he goes.
(3) An auto parts company sells defective parts at a lower cost and tells customers they are just older models.
(4) The customer of a large department store can't find anyone to help her and complains.
(5) A neighbor doesn't take care of his or her yard, which makes the whole neighborhood look bad.

30. Which of the following groups does not bear responsibility for the incident involving the Khian Sea?

(1) the U.S. government
(2) the boat's crew
(3) Gonaïves's residents
(4) the boat's owner
(5) large corporations

Questions 31–33 refer to the following chart, graph, and photograph.

SUBURBAN POPULATION DENSITY

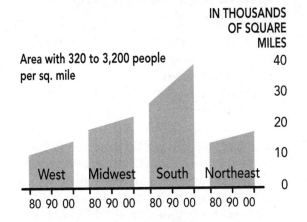

Percentage change in growth

	1980–1990	1990–2000
West	+23%	+7%
Midwest	+10%	+12%
South	+29%	+19%
Northwest	+15%	+7%

Source: US Census Bureau

31. Which of the following inferences can be made about the people who live in the houses in the picture?

(1) They have similar cultural backgrounds.
(2) They have similar jobs.
(3) They earn similar amounts of money.
(4) They have the same number of children.
(5) They have the same preference for climate.

32. According to the graph, where were the largest number of neighborhoods like the one in the picture in the year 2000?

(1) the Northeast
(2) the South
(3) the Northwest
(4) the West
(5) the Midwest

33. According to the chart, which of the following statements is true?

(1) The percentage of growth in western and midwestern suburbs increased between 1990 and 2000.
(2) The suburbs in the northeast and west shrank in size over the decade between 1990 and 2000.
(3) The decade between 1990 and 2000 witnessed the greatest rate of suburban growth in U.S. history.
(4) The growth rate of suburbs in the Midwest had slowed by the end of the twentieth century.
(5) By the end of the 20th century the suburban growth rate had slowed most dramatically in the West.

Questions 34–37 are based on the following labels applied to certain groups before, during, and after the Civil War.

Abolitionist—one who strongly favored the abolishing of slavery

Secessionist—one who favored slave states' breaking away from the Union

Confederate—one who joined in the cause of the southern states that seceded from the Union

Carpetbagger—a northerner who moved to the South during Reconstruction to take advantage of business and political opportunities.

Scalawag—a white southerner who supported the efforts of the North in rebuilding the South

34. General P. G. T. Beauregard, a former Confederate officer, supported the Union's efforts to reconcile after a long, bitter, bloody battle. What would he have been described by fellow Southerners as?

(1) an abolitionist
(2) a secessionist
(3) a confederate
(4) a carpetbagger
(5) a scalawag

35. A northern native who packed only what necessities he could carry and moved to the South after the war in search of get-rich-quick schemes was called which of the following?

(1) an abolitionist
(2) a secessionist
(3) a confederate
(4) a carpetbagger
(5) a scalawag

36. Someone who joined the Underground Railroad before and during the war to help slaves escape to the North or Canada was considered to be which of the following?

(1) an abolitionist
(2) a secessionist
(3) a confederate
(4) a carpetbagger
(5) a scalawag

37. Poor Appalachian whites who feuded with planters and who joined the reconstruction efforts as a way of retaliating against their former southern enemies were called which of the following?

(1) abolitionists
(2) secessionists
(3) confederates
(4) carpetbaggers
(5) scalawags

Questions 38–40 refer to the passage and photographs below.

During the early 1800s, proponents of two different models of prisons, the Auburn State Prison and the Eastern State Penitentiary, hotly debated their mutual merits and faults. Prisoners at the Auburn State Prison worked in complete silence during their confinement and slept in separate cells at night, while prisoners at Eastern State Penitentiary were kept in solitary confinement all day long. The idea behind the latter was that convicts would have time to contemplate the crime they had committed and repent. Modern prisons use elements of both models to rehabilitate prisoners. The photograph on the top shows convicts from a Georgia prison working on a quarry at the turn of the 20th century. The photograph on the bottom shows a visitor inspecting . . . solitary confinement cells.

38. The passage gives the rationale for the solitary confinement model. Which of the following would best explain the reasoning behind the Auburn State Prison model?

(1) Prisoners would be more physically and mentally healthy if they had the chance to work out of doors.
(2) Without at least some social life, prisoners would become more dangerous and likely to revolt.
(3) By working, prisoners would both learn discipline and contribute to the maintenance of the prison.
(4) Guards needed to be able to interact with prisoners, or they would quit their jobs out of boredom.
(5) Prisons would offer more employment opportunities for guards if prisoners required more supervision.

39. Which of the following examples of modern prison policy does not derive from one of the two practices described in the passage?

(1) When a prisoner misbehaves, he is transferred to a unit far from other prisoners.
(2) Prisoners have jobs within the prison in maintenance, service, and product manufacture.
(3) Prisoners can often take classes to improve their skills and further their education.
(4) Communication between prisoners is discouraged and carefully monitored by guards.
(5) Prisons have chaplains and counselors on staff to encourage self-reflection and rehabilitation.

40. What might the picture on the top have been used for?

(1) to assure people in nearby communities that prisoner escape was impossible
(2) to show prisoners' families that prisoners were receiving decent treatment
(3) to prove that prisoners were being sufficiently punished for their crimes
(4) to emphasize that the "work" model was not a "soft" approach to rehabilitation
(5) to demonstrate that prisoners had ample opportunity to reflect on their crimes

Questions 41 and 42 refer to the announcement below.

CURBSIDE RECYCLING

PAPER

Place in paper bag on top of or beside recycling bin

- Newspaper, with inserts
- Magazines/ Catalogs, phone books, paper back books (no hardcover books)
- Junk Mail
- Office and mixed paper/brown bags
- Paperboard, e.g. cracker, cereal boxes, remove liners
- Corrugated cardboard, flatten to 3'x 3' or smaller and place under or beside recycling bin.
- No soiled paper, gift wrap or plastic bags*
- No egg cartons or pizza boxes*
- * These items may be placed in your yellow city trash bag.

CONTAINERS

Rinse and place inside of recycling bin

- Glass bottles/jars, labels, neck rings, metal caps, corks, etc. may stay on. (No broken or other glass such as light bulbs, window or auto glass, dishes, glasses, Pyrex.)*
- Metal food cans, non-deposit and deposit cans aluminum foil, labels and metal caps may stay. May flatten to save space. (No paint or aerosol cans.)*
- All plastic bottles and jars, remove caps, lids & neck rings. Place on bottom of bin to prevent blowing away. (No motor oil containers or plastic bags. No plastic pails or buckets. No plastic other than containers.)*
- Milk and juice cartons and drink boxes, remove plastic and straws.
- * These items may be placed in your yellow city trash bag.

41. Which of the following should not be placed in the curbside recycling bin?

(1) rinsed tomato sauce cans
(2) torn birthday present wrapping
(3) supermarket advertising circulars
(4) plastic orange juice containers
(5) last year's phone book

42. What would the group of people who organized the recycling program in Worcester most likely consider themselves?

(1) capitalists
(2) pacifists
(3) immigrants
(4) human-rights activists
(5) environmentalists

Questions 43 and 44 refer to the Gettysburg Address, printed below.

Fourscore and seven years ago our fathers brought forth on this continent, a new nation, conceived in Liberty, and dedicated to the proposition that all men are created equal.

Now we are engaged in a great civil war, testing whether that nation or any nation so conceived and so dedicated, can long endure. We are met on a great battle-field of that war. We have come to dedicate a portion of that field as a final resting place for those who here gave their lives that that nation might live. It is altogether fitting and proper that we should do this.

But, in a larger sense, we cannot dedicate—we cannot consecrate—we cannot hallow—this ground. The brave men, living and dead, who struggled here, have consecrated it, far above our poor power to add or detract. The world will little note, nor long remember what we say here, but it can never forget what they did here. It is for us the living, rather, to be dedicated here to the unfinished work which they who fought here have thus far so nobly advanced. It is rather for us to be here dedicated to the great task remaining before us—that from these honored dead we take increased devotion to that cause for which they gave the last full measure of devotion—that we here highly resolve that these dead shall not have died in vain—that this nation, under God, shall have a new birth of freedom—and that government of the people, by the people, for the people, shall not perish from the earth.

—Abraham Lincoln, November 19, 1863, Gettysburg, Pennsylvania

43. What was Gettysburg?

    (1) a town on the border between the North and South
    (2) a major city in Pennsylvania during the 19th century
    (3) the site of a vicious battle during the Civil War
    (4) President Abraham Lincoln's hometown
    (5) a church where many people worshiped

44. What was the purpose of Lincoln's speech?

    (1) to inspire Americans to preserve their nation
    (2) to remember the names of all of the dead
    (3) to clarify the side that Lincoln took in the war
    (4) to retell the history of the United States
    (5) to announce the end of slavery

Question 45 refers to the following cartoon.

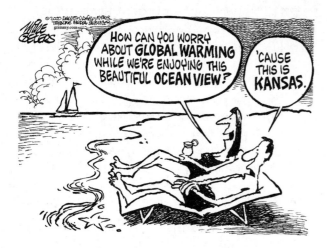

45. What is the point of this cartoon?

(1) Some people are so stressed out by their jobs that they can't enjoy their vacations.

(2) Global warming isn't a problem in the southern hemisphere and won't affect vacation resorts.

(3) Global warming is a serious problem if it means that Kansas might become a coastal state.

(4) Global warming is a figment of the imagination of people who worry too much about everything.

(5) Kansas will be the first state to feel the effects of global warming if no action is taken.

Questions 46–48 refer to the passage and map of the Gaza Strip in the Middle East.

The Gaza Strip, a hotly disputed area in the region once called Palestine, covers 140 square miles of rolling, dune-covered coastal plain with no surface water. It is a virtual desert with only 13 percent arable land, but with nearly 900,000 Palestinians and a handful of Jewish settlers it is also one of the most densely populated places in the world.

ISRAEL AND THE PALESTINIAN TERRITORIES, 2001

The following remarks were made by Alexandra Avakian, a photographer and journalist who lived in Gaza.

Seventy percent of the population here comes from refugee families, people who fled in 1948 from Israel's War of Independence. The poverty level is much higher than on the West Bank. The water in Gaza has a lot of salt, a lot of pollution. The aquifer is [salty] underneath the strip, and in the past Palestinians found it difficult to get permission to dig new wells. The 5,000 Israeli settlers who live in Gaza are sitting on the sweetest water, so when and if they ever leave, the Palestinians will have access to that.

The United Nations was doing the only infrastructural work in Gaza, and these problems were just not addressed. All these people . . . if you think about the Shati refugee camp, where 80,000 people are squeezed into less than a mile, living on top of each other, sanitation goes by the wayside pretty, pretty quickly.

Grandparents in every refugee camp in Gaza remember exactly where they came from before 1948. They remember their village. They'll talk about the well and the orchards, and how beautiful their home was. And now they're living in these thrown-together shacks made of cinder blocks and metal roofs, and often don't have running water, and the sewage is right outside the door.

—Excerpted from an interview with Alexandra Avakian, www.nationalgeographic.com/Gaza.

46. The map and/or passage support which of the following statements?

    (1) Most Palestinians have been living on the Gaza Strip for centuries.
    (2) Gaza would be a healthy place to live if there were better political organization.
    (3) Deserts are always far inland from oceans and cannot sustain human life.
    (4) Palestinians in Gaza are often homesick for the places from which they fled.
    (5) Palestinians and Israelis live together peacefully despite cramped conditions.

47. From the passage and the map, which of the following inferences can be made about the West Bank?

    (1) It is less important to Palestinians than Gaza.
    (2) It has a better water supply and sanitation system.
    (3) It is another settlement area for Palestinian refugees.
    (4) It is important to Palestinians for religious reasons.
    (5) It has a smaller population than Gaza.

48. Which of the following organizations would be *least* likely to become involved in addressing the living conditions in Gaza?

    (1) the World Conservation Monitoring Center (WCMC)
    (2) the United Nations High Commission for Refugees (UNHCR)
    (3) the Palestinian Liberation Organization (PLO)
    (4) the United Nations Food and Agriculture Organization (FAO)
    (5) the World Health Organization (WHO)

Questions 49 and 50 refer to the following passage.

Jamaica Plain began as a collection of farms and pretty suburban estates. In the mid-1800s, it evolved into one of Boston's renowned streetcar suburbs, a residential pocket in an expanding city. With the trolley and train came factory operatives as well as downtown professionals, roofers, masons, painters, and carpenters. [Jamaica Plain] soon offered something for nearly every pocketbook. Suburban homes with sizable yards were set cheek by jowl with brick townhouses. Queen Anne-style homes overlooked woodframe double and triple deckers, and the row houses of the blue-collared.

This housing diversity and the resulting mix of residents made [Jamaica Plain] unique among Boston neighborhoods. Each sub-neighborhood had a feeling of completeness about it. Children, families, and older retirees were out and about at all hours, walking babies or dogs, watching one another's children. There were places for students and for first time homebuyers ready to begin families or to settle near cousins, brothers, or grandparents. Most important, people could—and did—move up or down the economic scale without being forced to leave the community as their incomes and leisure interests changed. It wasn't at all uncommon to have lived at several addresses before settling down into a final home, yet never once leave Jamaica Plain's three-square-mile limits.

—Excerpted from "Building a Neighborhood" by Kathleen Hirsch, *Orion: People and Nature*, Winter 2001.

49. The passage about Jamaica Plain implies which of the following?

    (1) Having so many housing options within a single community is a positive feature.
    (2) Jamaica Plain is beginning to slide downhill because of an increase of racial tension.
    (3) In ten years Jamaica Plain will no longer be recognizable as the community it is today.
    (4) There have always been segments of Jamaica Plain's population that resisted the mix of social classes.
    (5) The author does not consider Jamaica Plain a particularly appealing place to live.

50. Who among the following would not be a likely resident of Jamaica Plain?

    (1) a doctor at one of Boston's hospitals
    (2) an electronics factory worker
    (3) a recent immigrant from Ecuador
    (4) a retired schoolteacher
    (5) a backwoods recluse

Answers are on pages 136–139.

Go to **www.GEDSocialStudies.com** for additional practice and instruction!

Chapter 3

Power, Authority, and Governance

GED Social Studies pages 183–215
Complete GED pages 327–398

Questions 1 and 2 refer to the cartoon below.

"How do I know what I think
until I see how the opinion
polls are going?"

1. What is the main idea of this cartoon?

    (1) Candidates base their opinions on
        those of the voting public.
    (2) Voters decide how they will vote after
        reading the polls.
    (3) Media surveys attempt to influence
        the people being polled.
    (4) Managers of political campaigns do
        not believe in opinion polls.
    (5) Public opinion is influenced by
        popular political candidates.

2. In which of the following situations might
    the cartoonist have drawn the politician in
    the cartoon to resemble an actual political
    candidate?

    If that candidate
    (1) took a strong stand in favor of
        increased taxes and didn't back down
        when many voters voiced their
        disapproval
    (2) withdrew from the race for governor
        because the press revealed he or she
        had had an affair with an aide
    (3) buckled under the weight of public
        opinion and changed his or her
        position on environmental protection
    (4) accused his or her opponents of not
        having any new ideas about how to
        solve important problems
    (5) won the election and then did exactly
        the opposite of what he or she had
        said regarding the economy

Questions 3–5 are based on the following passage.

Did you know that the government can force U.S. citizens to sell their property? The right of eminent domain gives city, state, and federal government the power to take property from an owner if the seizure is done for a public purpose and if a fair price is offered. Governments have generally used eminent domain to acquire unsafe property that they wished to condemn or to acquire land for government projects.

In one unusual case, the California Supreme Court ruled that the City of Oakland could use the power of eminent domain to keep the Raiders football team from moving to Los Angeles. Higher courts later overturned that ruling on the grounds that football is not primarily a public activity.

Current debate over eminent domain mainly involves environmental regulations that severely limit how land can be used. These regulations do not take land from anyone, but government critics argue that something valuable has been taken nonetheless when developers are not allowed to build on their land or farmers are not allowed to drain their fields.

3. Which of the following is an improper application of the right of eminent domain?

   (1) A city pays several homeowners the appraised market value of their houses in order to gain space for expansion of a school.
   (2) A city offers to purchase many acres of farmland at a fair price, against an owner's wishes, in order to build an airport.
   (3) A state buys land from a large corporation at a mutually agreed upon price in order to establish a state park.
   (4) A state pays a premium price for land it intends to resell at a later time to private parties for a profit.
   (5) The federal government buys a huge tract of land from unwilling but well-paid sellers in order to extend a national park.

4. What do the critics of environmental regulations regarding land use want the government to do?

   (1) exempt developers and farmers from environmental regulations
   (2) return the land taken by these regulations to the original owners
   (3) pay landowners for any decrease in their property value caused by regulation
   (4) eliminate environmental regulations regarding how land is used
   (5) grant environmental groups ownership of the regulated lands

5. Which value are government officials allowing to take precedence when they apply their power of eminent domain?

   (1) the government's show of power over private ownership
   (2) the power of the federal over the local government
   (3) the welfare of a few over the financial concern of many
   (4) the public good over the rights of the individual
   (5) the private owners' rights over the public's pleasure

Questions 6 and 7 refer to the following passage.

"Mister," said an African American from Chicago, discussing his vote with me in 1960, "they could put a dog at the head of that ticket and if they called him Democratic I'd vote for him. This hoolarium about civil rights doesn't mean anything to me—it's the man who puts money into my pocket that counts."

6. From this quote you can infer which of the following?

   (1) The speaker is convinced that civil rights activists have hurt the cause of minorities.
   (2) The speaker has seen civil right activists pressure politicians for jobs for minorities.
   (3) The speaker believes that Democrats have improved economic conditions for minorities.
   (4) The speaker has been frequently bribed by Democrats to vote for them in elections.
   (5) The speaker thinks that more Democrats should join the Civil Rights movement.

7. On which of the following does the man being quoted place a high value?

   (1) financial security
   (2) political loyalty
   (3) racial equality
   (4) civil liberties
   (5) moral standards

8. Many opponents of gun-control legislation refer to a constitutional amendment to support their cause. Which of the following is the best legal argument in favor of gun-control legislation?

   (1) Guns don't kill people; people kill people, so people need to be instructed not to use guns inappropriately.
   (2) If guns could be easily obtained and everyone were armed, crime would automatically decrease tenfold.
   (3) A greater number of deaths are caused by handguns in the United States than in any other industrialized nation.
   (4) The right to bear arms applied only when colonial America had no standing army and armed citizens formed the militia.
   (5) Owners of handguns run a higher risk of having their weapons turned against them than those who don't own a gun.

9. Separation of church and state as described in the U.S. Constitution is often cited as the reason for prohibiting all except which of the following?

   (1) displaying the Nativity scene on public property
   (2) prayer time in the public schools
   (3) inclusion of religious symbols, such as the cross, on government flags
   (4) election of an ordained minister to public office
   (5) teaching creationism and excluding the theory of evolution in public schools

Questions 10–12 are based on the first constitutional amendment, the bar graph, and the passage below.

Amendment I: Congress shall make no law respecting an establishment of religion, or prohibiting the free exercise thereof; or abridging the freedom of speech, or of the press; or the right of the people peaceably to assemble, and to petition the Government for a redress of grievances.

Speech That Should Be Restricted

A poll of 1,026 Americans taken between July 17 and August 1, 1997, found that 93 percent would vote for the First Amendment if it were being ratified in 1997. However, according to those polled, some forms of speech should be restricted:

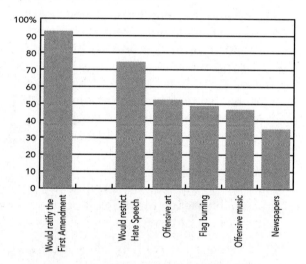

Source: Center for Survey Research and Analysis, 1997.

Free speech is vital to the attainment and advancement of knowledge, and the search for the truth. The eminent 19th century writer and civil libertarian, John Stuart Mill, contended that enlightened judgment is possible only if one considers all facts and ideas, from whatever source, and tests one's own conclusion against opposing views. Therefore, all points of view—even those that are "bad" or socially harmful—should be represented in society's "marketplace of ideas."

Free speech is necessary to our system of self-government and gives the American people a "checking function" against government excess and corruption. If the American people are to be the masters of their fate and of their elected government,

they must be well-informed and have access to all information, ideas and points of view. Mass ignorance is a breeding ground for oppression and tyranny.

—Excerpted from "Freedom of Expression", *Civil Liberties: Opposing Viewpoints*, American Civil Liberties Union

10. According to the people who were polled, which form of free speech is of the greatest concern?

(1) newspapers
(2) offensive art
(3) flag burning
(4) hate speech
(5) offensive music

11. Which of the following statements best summarizes the point of view expressed in the passage?

(1) Free speech is important because even nineteenth-century philosophers thought so.
(2) A true democracy requires unlimited opportunities for its citizens to be informed.
(3) The marketplace of ideas should include everything except racism and pornography.
(4) Because of free speech, our government officials can be as corrupt as they want to be.
(5) Free speech is what makes America different from and superior to the rest of the world.

12. Which of the following people would be likely to favor restricting freedom of speech?

(1) an artist whose work has offended church members
(2) a neo-Nazi who publishes a newspaper that denigrates Jews
(3) an anti-war demonstrator who burns the American flag in protest
(4) a researcher concerned about the link between pornography and violence
(5) a rap musician whose lyrics are considered inappropriate for children.

Questions 13–16 are based on the following amendments to the U.S. Constitution.

Fourteenth Amendment—All persons born or naturalized in the United States, and subject to the jurisdiction thereof, are citizens of the United States and of the State wherein they reside. No State shall make or enforce any law which shall abridge the privileges or immunities of citizens of the United States; nor shall any State deprive any person of life, liberty, or property, without due process of law; nor deny to any person within its jurisdiction the equal protection of the laws.

Fifteenth Amendment—The right of citizens of the United States to vote shall not be denied or abridged by the United States or by any State on account of race, color, or previous condition of servitude.

Nineteenth Amendment—The right of citizens of the United States to vote shall not be denied or abridged by the United States or by any State on account of sex.

Twenty-Fourth Amendment—The right of citizens of the United States to vote in any primary or other election for President or Vice President, for electors for President or Vice President, or for Senator or Representative in Congress, shall not be denied or abridged by the United States or any State by reason of failure to pay any poll tax or other tax.

Twenty-Sixth Amendment—The right of citizens of the United States, who are eighteen years of age or older, to vote shall not be denied or abridged by the United States or by any State on account of age.

13. What does charging a tax for the privilege of voting in order to keep certain citizens from voting imply about those citizens?

    (1) They cannot afford to pay such a tax.
    (2) They do not fulfill their financial obligations.
    (3) They would not vote anyway.
    (4) They are ignorant of constitutional law.
    (5) They are not full citizens in the eyes of the law.

14. The amendments to the U.S. Constitution are listed in numerical and chronological order. Based on this information, which of the following is true? The right to vote was granted to

    (1) white women before African American men or women
    (2) African American men before women of any color
    (3) African Americans before they were legally declared citizens
    (4) eighteen-year-old males before eighteen-year-old females
    (5) eighteen-year-old whites before eighteen-year-old blacks

15. Many citizens protested state laws requiring a person to be twenty-one or older to be able to vote. After all, some of these citizens who were under the age of twenty-one could be drafted, get married, and enter into certain business transactions. This protest resulted in which of the following amendments?

    (1) the Fourteenth Amendment
    (2) the Fifteenth Amendment
    (3) the Nineteenth Amendment
    (4) the Twenty-Fourth Amendment
    (5) the Twenty-Sixth Amendment

16. One way in which many states circumvented the federal laws requiring them to allow African Americans and women to vote was to charge a duty, payable by election day, to anyone wishing to exercise his or her constitutional right. Which of the following amendments outlawed this practice?

    (1) the Fourteenth Amendment
    (2) the Fifteenth Amendment
    (3) the Nineteenth Amendment
    (4) the Twenty-Fourth Amendment
    (5) the Twenty-Sixth Amendment

U.S. Department of Justice
Immigration and Naturalization Service

Application for Employment Authorization

Do Not Write in This Block

Remarks	Action Stamp	Fee Stamp
A#		
Applicant is filing under §274a.12 _____		

☐ Application Approved. Employment Authorized / Extended (Circle One)   until _____ (Date).
_____ (Date).

Subject to the following conditions: _____

☐ Application Denied.
    ☐ Failed to establish eligibility under 8 CFR 274a.12 (a) or (c).
    ☐ Failed to establish economic necessity as required in 8 CFR 274a. 12(c) (14), (18) and 8 CFR 214.2(f)

I am applying for:
    ☐ Permission to accept employment
    ☐ Replacement (of lost employment authorization document).
    ☐ Renewal of my permission to accept employment (attach previous employment authorization document).

1. Name (Family Name in CAPS) (First) (Middle)

2. Other Names Used (Include Maiden Name)

3. Address in the United States (Number and Street) (Apt. Number)

(Town or City) (State/Country) (ZIP Code)

4. Country of Citizenship/Nationality

5. Place of Birth (Town or City) (State/Province) (Country)

6. Date of Birth (Month/Day/Year)   7. Sex ☐ ☐

8. Marital Status   ☐ Married   ☐ Single
               ☐ Widowed   ☐ Divorced

9. Social Security Number (Include all numbers you have ever used) (if any)

10. Alien Registration Number (A-Number) or 1-94 Number (if any)

11. Have you ever before applied for employment authorization from INS?
☐ **Yes** (if yes, complete below)   ☐ **No**
Which INS Office?   Date(s)

Results (Granted or Denied - attach all documentation)

12. Date of Last Entry into the U.S. (Month/Day/Year)

13. Place of Last Entry into the U.S.

14. Manner of Last Entry (Visitor, Student, etc.)

15. Current Immigration Status (Visitor, Student, etc.)

16. Go to Part 2 of the instructions, Eligibility Categories. In the space below, place the letter and the number of the category you selected from the instructions (For example, (a)(8), (c)(17)(iii), etc.).

Eligibility under 8 CFR 274a.12

(   ) (   ) (   )

Certification

Your Certification: I certify, under penalty of perjury under the laws of the United States of America, that the foregoing is true and correct. Furthermore, I authorize the release of any information which the immigration and Naturalization Service needs to determine eligibility for the benefit I am seeking. I have read the instructions in Part 2 and have identified the appropriate eligibility category in Block 16.

Signature   Telephone Number   Date

Signature of Person Preparing Form, If Other Than Above: I declare that this document was prepared by me at the request of the applicant and is based on all information of which I have any knowledge.

Print Name   Address   *Signature*   Date

Initial Receipt	Resubmitted	Relocated		Completed		
		Rec'd	Sent	Approved	Denied	Returned

Questions 17–20 refer to the application for employment authorization on page 42.

17. Who of the following would *not* need to fill out this form if he or she wanted to work in the United States?

    (1) a refugee from a war-torn country
    (2) a student from Spain or Greece
    (3) the Jamaican wife of an American-born husband
    (4) a Haitian immigrant
    (5) the American-born wife of an Iranian husband

18. Which piece of information is *not* necessary to complete this form?

    (1) the city of arrival in United States
    (2) previous employers in country of origin
    (3) documentation from past applications
    (4) "Green card" (alien registration) number
    (5) permission to release information

19. According to the application form, which of the following consequences could *not* result from filing it?

    (1) The application could be approved, thereby authorizing the applicant's employment in the United States until a particular date.
    (2) The application could be approved, thereby extending permission for the applicant to work in the United States until a particular date.
    (3) The application could be approved but only under certain conditions which the applicant would have to meet in order to work.
    (4) The application could be voided and a new one required because of bureaucratic mishandling.
    (5) The application could be denied because the applicant failed to demonstrate an economic need to work in the United States.

20. Which of the following employers would be *least* likely to require this employment authorization form from its immigrant workers?

    (1) a large retail chain store currently under government scrutiny for alleged hiring misconduct
    (2) a high-tech company seeking engineers and software experts to design a new product
    (3) a factory manager who pays workers less than minimum wage and gives them cash "under the table"
    (4) a state governor eager to demonstrate to voters that she has an ethnically diverse cabinet of advisors
    (5) the school department in an urban area that needs bilingual teachers for new students from other countries

Questions 21 and 22 are based on the following short passage.

Canada has used the Maple Leaf as a symbol for its flag only since February of 1965. Before that, the country had flown the Red Ensign for 20 years. Although it had replaced the British Union Jack, the Red Ensign still incorporated the Union Jack into its basic design. The Maple Leaf was the first flag of Canada that truly proclaimed its sovereignty from Great Britain.

21. From the context in which it is used, what can we infer that the term *sovereignty* means?

    (1) development
    (2) alliance
    (3) alienation
    (4) patriotism
    (5) independence

22. Which of the following statements is adequately supported by the passage?

    (1) Canada was under the rule of France during the 17th and 18th centuries.
    (2) Canada first received a degree of sovereignty from Great Britain in 1867.
    (3) Canada's citizens voted their disapproval of the Red Ensign.
    (4) Canada's historical ties to Great Britain extend back many years.
    (5) Canada is a country that has never had much national pride.

Questions 23 and 24 refer to the following chart.

YEAR	LAW	PURPOSE
1882	Chinese Exclusion Act	to exclude Chinese immigrants
1917	Anarchist Act	to exclude subversive aliens
1953	Refugee Relief Act	to allow entry for war refugees from communist countries or Middle East
1965	Amendments to the Immigration and Nationality Acts	to abolish quotas based on national origin and set up occupation-related hardship categories
1980	Refugee Act	to increase number of allowable immigrants and redefine the word "refugee"

23. In general, what has the purpose of the United States immigration laws over the years been?

    (1) to exclude certain races from entering the United States
    (2) to allow the largest numbers of immigrants possible into the United States
    (3) to increase restrictions on the number of immigrants to the United States
    (4) to control the types of people who could immigrate into the United States
    (5) to eliminate the need for quotas in future immigration laws

24. Which of the laws mentioned would have had the most impact on the fate of a Soviet dissident in 1957?

    (1) the 1882 Chinese Exclusion Act
    (2) the 1917 Anarchist Act
    (3) the 1953 Refugee Relief Act
    (4) the 1965 amendments to the Immigration and Nationality Acts
    (5) the 1980 Refugee Act

Question 25 refers to the photograph and brief passage below.

Imperial troops fired on peaceful demonstrators in Saint Petersburg in January 1905. Rage over "Bloody Sunday" spread across Russia, developing into a revolution. Czar Nicholas II was forced to allow the creation of a legislative assembly and to grant citizens important civil rights.

25. Which of the following was *not* a belief held by the Russian Czar in 1905?

   (1) His troops could hurt and kill unarmed people.
   (2) He could control the will of the people by force.
   (3) Granting citizens civil rights was not a good idea.
   (4) People would get angry at his actions and revolt.
   (5) Attacking people in the street was a good scare tactic.

Questions 26 and 27 refer to the passage below.

In a sense, Nixon was the victim of circumstances. The Watergate scandal took place within the context of an even more significant development which went back to the Great Depression and World War II. Since those years, presidents have assumed broader powers to deal with national emergencies. And in the 1970's, President Lyndon Johnson, and then President Nixon, claimed broader powers to wage war in Vietnam. Both Nixon and Johnson often chose to ignore Congress when Congress felt it had the right to be consulted on the conduct of the war. By the mid-1970's many observers in Congress and elsewhere feared that the office of chief executive had become "the imperial presidency." It was Nixon who bore the full brunt of those who sought to restrain the presidency.

—Excerpted from *Politics, Power, and People* by Thomas Raynor

26. From the context in which it is used, what can *imperial* be understood to mean?

   (1) democratic
   (2) weak
   (3) communistic
   (4) unappealing
   (5) authoritarian

27. Which of the following actions by a president could be interpreted as having gone beyond the powers delegated to the office by the Constitution in a way similar to that attributed to Johnson and Nixon?

   (1) Bill Clinton's extramarital affair with a White House intern
   (2) George W. Bush's decision to set up military tribunals to try terrorists
   (3) Thomas Jefferson's suspension of trade with France and England
   (4) Abraham Lincoln's "Emancipation Proclamation" that freed the slaves
   (5) Grover Cleveland's injunction against striking Pullman car workers

Questions 28–30 are based on the following quote from the Monroe Doctrine.

With the existing colonies and dependencies of any European Power we have not interfered and shall not interfere. But with the governments who have declared their independence and maintained it, and whose independence we have, on great consideration and just principles acknowledged, we could not view any interposition for the purpose of oppressing them, or controlling in any other manner their destiny, by any European Power, in any other light than a manifestation of an unfriendly disposition towards the United States.

28. Which of the following historical events did the U.S. government view as a display of an "unfriendly disposition toward the United States" as defined by the Monroe Doctrine?

(1) the victory of the Liberal Party over the Conservatives in Canada in the 1940s
(2) the ousting of President Juan Perón by a military coup in Argentina in the 1950s
(3) the building up of offensive nuclear missiles in Cuba by Russia in the 1960s
(4) the pro-independence, anti-American demonstrations in Puerto Rico in the 1970s
(5) the arrival by boat of Cuban prisoners on United States shores in the 1980s

29. Which of the following foreign policy terms most closely describes the Monroe Doctrine?

(1) **imperialism** – the policy of one nation's extending its authority over other territories or nations
(2) **isolationism**—the policy of noninterference in world affairs
(3) **nationalism**—the belief that the welfare of one's own nation must be put ahead of that of others
(4) **jingoism**—a policy of extreme nationalism characterized by frequent threats of warlike actions
(5) **internationalism**—the position that one nation's actions affect every other nation

30. Which of the following interpretations of the Monroe Doctrine by a U.S. president did Latin American governments view unfavorably?

(1) James Polk's warning against diplomatic and armed interference in the Americas by outside countries
(2) Grover Cleveland's use of the doctrine to help settle a boundary dispute between Venezuela and British Guiana
(3) Theodore Roosevelt's proclamation that the United States would intervene in the affairs of a Latin American government if it were threatened by European interference
(4) Franklin Roosevelt's "good neighbor policy" that gave expression to the idea that all American countries share similar community interests
(5) John Kennedy's development of the Alliance for Progress that promised technical and financial cooperation among American nations

Questions 31–33 refer to the following graph.

REPORTED VOTING BY RACE AND ETHNICITY
Presidential Elections 1976-1996

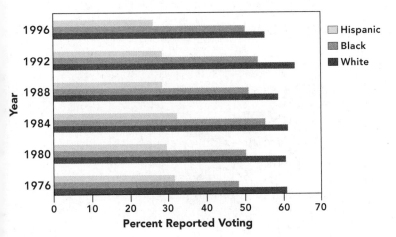

31. Which of the following statements is accurate based on the information in the graph?

    (1) The reason there have always been white presidents is because a greater percentage of whites vote than other groups.

    (2) More African Americans voted in 1988 than in any of the other presidential election years between 1976 and 1996.

    (3) The percentage of African Americans who voted in presidential elections between 1976 and 1996 is consistently more than 50%.

    (4) A greater percentage of whites voted in the elections between 1976 and 1996 than either of the two other major groups.

    (5) In 1984 more Hispanics voted than in other years because there was a Hispanic vice-presidential candidate.

32. Which of the following people would be most troubled by the information presented in the graph?

    (1) a political reporter from a major city newspaper

    (2) a white political candidate from a state that is mostly white

    (3) a Hispanic congressman who is well-liked by his white constituents

    (4) Japanese investors observing the elections from overseas

    (5) an African American candidate whose position would benefit all minorities.

33. What might you predict the graph of the 2000 presidential election to look like?

    (1) It would not look much different from those of previous years, especially since a conservative white Republican won the race.

    (2) It would show a sharp decline in the percentage of Hispanic voters because fewer Hispanics immigrated to the United States in 2000 than earlier.

    (3) It would show an enormous increase in the percentages of all voters because of the increase in voter-registration drives.

    (4) It would show a significant increase in African American and Hispanic voters even though there were no minority candidates.

    (5) It would show a sharp decrease in white voters because of strong, prejudicial attitudes toward minority candidates.

34. The AARP (American Association for Retired Persons) is the largest special-interest group in the United States and is still growing. Now that one out of nine Americans are dues-paying members and the elderly population is growing more than twice as fast as the rest of the population, certain political issues have come to the forefront. Which of the following would most likely be the lowest priority of the AARP lobby?

    (1) Social Security cost-of-living increases

    (2) Medicare's paying for prescription drugs

    (3) federally subsidized child day-care centers

    (4) government-sponsored nursing-home care

    (5) regulations against age discrimination in employment

Questions 35–37 refer to the map and cartoon below. Both refer to the progress toward women's suffrage, or voting rights, in the United States. The cartoon was published in 1920, one year after women gained the constitutional right to vote. The map shows the years in which women were allowed to vote in individual states, and the types of elections in which women could participate.

WOMEN'S SUFFRAGE IN THE UNITED STATES

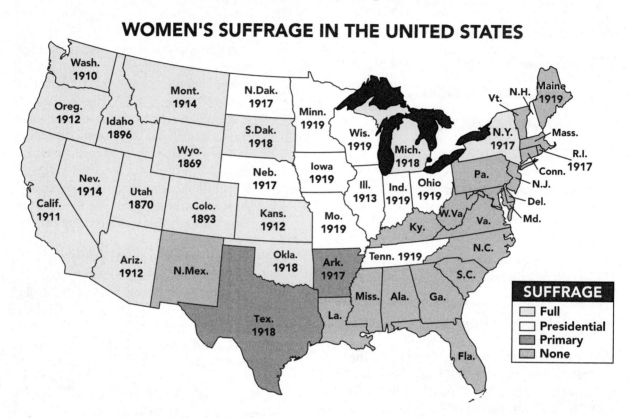

35. It is evident from the cartoon that its artist perceived which of the following?

(1) that most women in 1920 were overweight

(2) that politicians were not respectful of women's ideas

(3) that Democrats and Republicans didn't like each other

(4) that women's ignorance about politics would cause problems

(5) that women voters could have a significant political impact

—Courtesy of BoondocksNet.com

36. In which of the following states could you have voted in the presidential election of 1908 if you were a woman?

(1) Oregon
(2) Wyoming
(3) Georgia
(4) Pennsylvania
(5) California

37. It is interesting to note that the states in the western part of the country all permitted women to vote prior to the passing of the Constitutional amendment in 1919. Which of the following is the most logical explanation for this phenomenon?

(1) The western states wanted to form their own government with women as leaders.
(2) Most women in the Eastern and Midwestern states had no interest in voting.
(3) The West was newly settled and not as tightly tied to political traditions as the East.
(4) The president had issued an edict that forbade women in the eastern United States to vote.
(5) Men in the eastern United States respected women so much that they didn't want them "dirtied" by politics.

Question 38 refers to the following picture.

38. Who are the people in this picture most likely to be?

(1) corporate executives gathering to support their employees
(2) long-time American citizens looking for work during the Depression
(3) anti-union strikebreakers threatening striking workers
(4) recent immigrant laborers requesting better work conditions
(5) supporters of an Italian politician running for public office

Questions 39–41 are based on the following passage.

Addressing four thousand naturalized citizens at Philadelphia in May 1915, Woodrow Wilson, the twenty-seventh president of the United States, expressed his belief that the immigrant served the unique purpose of constantly reminding the American citizen that this was a nation dedicated to the principle of equality of opportunity and justice for all. Just three days before this speech was given, the *Lusitania* had been sunk by the Germans with the loss of 1,198 lives. It was expected that Wilson in this, his first major speech after the tragedy, would call for immediate retaliation. Instead, he spoke of America as the example of peace, for "peace is the healing and elevating influence of the world and strife is not." He suggested that a great nation must be "too proud to fight." It was only after a time that most people realized that his arguments held a significance far surpassing easy thought of revenge.

39. According to this passage, which of the following can we infer to have been most highly valued by Woodrow Wilson?

(1) equality of opportunity
(2) justice for all people
(3) national pride
(4) peace in the world
(5) revenge at any cost

40. What opinion about Woodrow Wilson is suggested by this passage?

(1) Wilson spoke of America as an example of peace.
(2) Wilson was an eloquent and forceful speaker.
(3) Wilson believed America to be a nation of opportunity and justice.
(4) Wilson should have retaliated against the Germans immediately.
(5) Wilson was wise not to seek quick revenge against the Germans.

41. Which is a more recent example of a president of the United States choosing peace over strife?

(1) Bush's liberation of Kuwait from Iraq in the Gulf War
(2) Kennedy's ordering of a blockade of Cuba to keep Russians out
(3) Johnson's escalation of the war in Vietnam to save face for the United States
(4) Carter's initial refusal to send troops to rescue American hostages in Iran
(5) Ford's pardoning of Nixon for any role in the Watergate scandal

 Go to **www.GEDSocialStudies.com** for additional practice and instruction!

Questions 42–44 refer to the map and passage below.

1820 MAP OF THE EASTERN INDIAN NATIONS

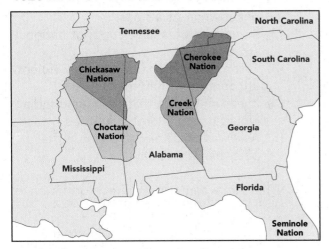

When Europeans first colonized North America, each settlement recognized its neighboring Indian tribes as self-governing, independent entities. The settlers negotiated treaties with Indians to secure peace and regulate trade and the expansion of white settlements. After the Revolutionary War, the U.S. Constitution gave Congress "plenary" power over all tribes. [Even so], Congress continued to recognize Indian tribes as nations and negotiated treaties with them as equal governments.

Federal policy toward America's native residents changed, however, when Andrew Jackson—renowned for his military campaign against the Indians—became president in 1829. The Indian Removal Act of 1830 required most of the eastern tribes to give up their lands and move west of the Mississippi River, despite any guarantees of permanent residence in their existing treaties with the government. When the Cherokees sued the state of Georgia in 1831 to prevent the enforcement of the act, the U.S. Supreme Court ruled in favor of the state, declaring that Indian tribes were "domestic dependent nations" that had lost their status as independent, foreign nations. Forty years later, Congress enacted legislation that changed the status of the tribes forever; the new law (known as Section 71) eliminated

the need for treaties with the Indian nations altogether by allowing Congress to use legislation—which did not require the Indians' consent—to govern the tribes.

—Excerpted from the introduction to *Native American Rights*, published by Current Controversies

42. From the context in which it is used, what can *plenary* be understood to mean?

(1) useless
(2) minimal
(3) complete
(4) unpredictable
(5) humorous

43. From the map and the passage, which of the following can be inferred about the white settlers in Alabama in 1818?

(1) They were in constant conflict with their Chickasaw neighbors.
(2) They would have been likely to have voted for Jackson in 1829.
(3) They were constantly afraid of attacks by the Seminole nation.
(4) They coexisted peacefully with a number of different tribal groups.
(5) They were beginning to adopt the ways of life of nearby Indian nations.

44. By declaring that Indian peoples were "domestic dependent nations" the U.S. Supreme Court set the stage for all except which of the following?

(1) a warm welcome to Indians as newly approved American citizens
(2) increasing public contempt and disregard for native people
(3) a mass exodus of Native Americans to the Midwestern plains
(4) a disruption in the unique cultural life of numerous tribes
(5) the dislocation of most Native Americans to reservations

Questions 45 and 46 refer to following passage.

One speaks uneasily of nations, or even of empires in Asia, other than the European empires created there, because it is not clear that what in the past existed there were nations or empires in any sense useful to contemporary political discussion. China was a civilization ruled by a centralized bureaucracy. It may from our anachronistic viewpoint be considered either an empire or nation; but surely the Chinese were not conscious of being other than the inevitable order of things.

It seems better to say that in Asia there were and are civilizations, agrarian, cultural, moral in quality, each with self-sufficient political existence; but not in the past a national existence; and certainly they were innocent of nationalism. They were aware of themselves as specific political entities only on those distant frontiers where other civilizations were encountered—or, more often, "barbarians," inferior in culture and political strength. These were either to be conquered, forced into submission and tribute, or assimilated. China and India both experienced "barbarian" conquest by nomads from Central Asia, the Manchus and Moghuls. Neither yielded its own identity or cultural autonomy, but "civilized" and thereby conquered the invaders, making the Manchus into Chinese and the Moghuls Indians—higher forms of mankind, as all eventually were willing to believe.

—Excerpted from *The Wrath of Nations: Civilization and the Furies of Nationalism* by William Pfaff

45. What is the purpose of this passage?

To suggest that

(1) the modern concept of "nation" was unknown in Asia's past
(2) Asian countries have superior national structures
(3) China and India had extremely violent encounters with nomads
(4) it was inevitable that China and India would become large countries
(5) Asia was politically stronger in the past than it is today

46. What can we infer from the information in the passage?

(1) Today there are many nomads still roaming Asia in search of civilizations to invade and overthrow.
(2) In central Asia there is a region characterized by the Moghul culture that is shared by many Indians.
(3) In what is today called China there are many people who trace their ancestry back to the Manchus.
(4) The centralized bureaucracy that used to be ancient China is very different since it changed into a nation.
(5) The Manchus and Moghuls have resented the Chinese and Indians ever since they failed to conquer them.

Questions 47 and 48 refer to the following passage.

In 2000 the Supreme Court narrowly ruled in the case of *The Boy Scouts of America v. Dale* to allow the Boy Scouts organization to discriminate against gay Scouts. James Dale, a former scout leader and homosexual, had challenged the constitutionality of the group's anti-gay membership policy. However, while the decision would appear to be a victory for the Scouts, its actual effect has been to drive away many long-time sponsors and supporters. In the months following the decision, much of the public recoiled at the Boy Scouts of America's betrayal of the group's long-held promise of being "open to all boys." Across the country, parents, funders, and Scouts themselves have begun to explore ways to dissociate themselves from the discrimination, reverse the anti-gay policy, and better support gay youth.

—Adapted from "All Tied Up in Knots" by Jennifer Grissom, *Lambda Update*, Fall 2000

47. According to the author of the passage, which of the following is true?

(1) The Supreme Court decision in favor of the Boy Scouts of America had a devastating effect on the gay-rights movement.

(2) James Dale is currently serving a lengthy prison sentence for challenging the policies of the Boys Scouts of America.

(3) This case attracted considerable media attention because the Boy Scouts of America have a reputation they wanted to protect.

(4) The backlash of the Boy Scouts' court victory is that people are aware of and disturbed by their discrimination policy.

(5) The majority of the judges on the Supreme Court that decided this case were clearly anti-gay and themselves discriminatory.

48. From the passage, what can you infer about the constitutional rights of homosexuals?

(1) They do not apply within privately operated organizations.

(2) They are likely to be ignored for many years to come.

(3) They have allowed gay people to lead lives free of discrimination.

(4) They are a priority of the U.S. Supreme Court.

(5) They differ widely from state to state.

Questions 49 and 50 are based on the short passage and map below.

The British Empire, established over the course of three centuries, began in the late 16th century with chartered commercial ventures in sugar and tobacco plantations, slave trading, and missionary activities in North America and the Caribbean Islands. During the late 19th and 20th centuries, the British Empire reached the height of its power, ruling over large parts of Africa, Asia, and North America.

BRITISH EMPIRE, EARLY 20th CENTURY

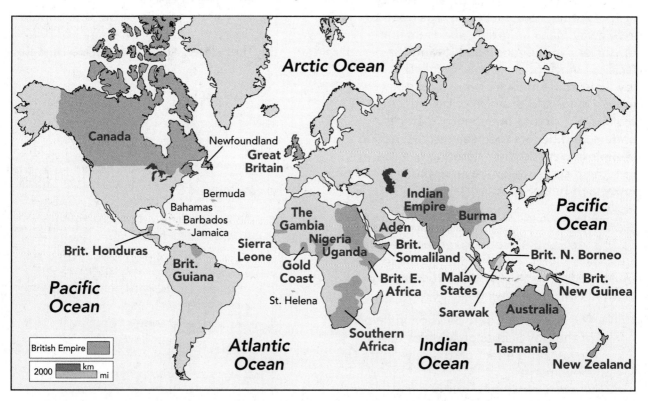

49. From the map and the passage what can you understand about the British Empire?

  (1) It had a strong presence in Eastern Europe.
  (2) It was known for its humanitarian policies.
  (3) Its reasons for expanding were strictly religious.
  (4) Its influence stretched across the entire globe.
  (5) Its African colonies were the first to rebel.

50. Which of the following would probably *not* have been found in a country ruled by the British Empire?

  (1) English tea
  (2) English money
  (3) an English climate
  (4) people speaking English
  (5) English-style clothing

Answers are on pages 139–142.

Chapter 4

Production, Distribution, and Consumption

GED Social Studies pages 217–251
Complete GED pages 399–426

Questions 1 and 2 are based on the following passage.

Though the United States and most of Europe experienced an industrial revolution during the latter half of the nineteenth century, the tremendous change from manual production to mechanical did not affect much of the Third World until recent years. As a result, many of the problems associated with industrialization have not affected these countries until recently. Now countries like South Korea are finding their workers objecting violently to long hours and low pay. The end result is that while the influence of labor organizations is at a low point in Japan and the United States, unions are increasing in power in South Korea. The power of labor organizations has increased to such an extent that they can stop the flow of work and, therefore, the flow of capital in a still-struggling economy.

1. What judgment does the author of the above passage make about Third World labor unions?

   The unions could
   (1) cripple the developing economies of their own countries
   (2) damage the economies of other industrialized countries
   (3) raise wages unreasonably high for laborers in their own countries
   (4) lengthen working hours for laborers in their own countries
   (5) worsen the working conditions for laborers in all countries

2. What unstated assumption does the author make?

   (1) Industrialization inevitably causes low wages and long hours.
   (2) Industrialization can be expected to increase wages for laborers in manufacturing.
   (3) Industrialization did not come to Third World countries such as South Korea until recently.
   (4) In South Korea, labor unions are beneficial to workers, but not to the nation's economy.
   (5) Industrialization does not necessarily have to mean mechanization.

Questions 3–5 are based on the following cartoon.

3. What is the cartoonist expressing an opinion about?

(1) the hog market
(2) farmers' problems
(3) a football strike
(4) drug use in sports
(5) sports fans

4. What is the cartoonist's opinion about owners and players?

(1) Owners are greedy; players are not.
(2) Owners are not greedy, but players are.
(3) Owners and players are greedy.
(4) Owners take advantage of players.
(5) Owners are not respected by players.

5. Which of the following is a conclusion that can be supported by the cartoon?

(1) If owners knew how negative their image was, they would give the players more money.
(2) If players knew how negative their image was, they would not ask for so much more money.
(3) If owners and players could work together, they could all become much wealthier.
(4) If owners and players could both earn more money, they would be earning reasonable incomes.
(5) If players and owners want to solve their problems, they should both give in on money demands.

Questions 6–8 are based on the following statement.

In a pastoral letter on the U.S. economy in 1986, several U.S. Roman Catholic bishops wrote that "foreign investors, attracted by low wages in less developed countries, should consider both the potential loss of jobs in the home country and the potential exploitation of workers in the host country."

6. To which of the following groups would this statement best apply?

(1) Third World labor unions striking for higher wages for factory work
(2) international corporations hiring cheap foreign labor to manufacture products
(3) American workers who protest the use of foreign labor to replace them
(4) missionaries in foreign countries who support the rights of workers there
(5) Third World governments that demand fair labor practices from foreign investors

7. In its statement, the committee of American Catholic bishops supported which value?

(1) private profit over nationalism
(2) nationalism over private profit
(3) economic fairness over private profit
(4) private profit over economic fairness
(5) economic fairness over nationalism

8. Which of the situations described below best illustrates a violation of the Catholic bishops' view?

(1) Union Carbide, an American chemical company, operating a plant in India
(2) General Motors' operating an automated automobile plant in Japan
(3) Coca-Cola Company's operating a state-of-the-art bottling plant in Australia
(4) McDonald Corporation's permitting franchises to operate in South Africa
(5) Royal Dutch Shell's operating gas stations in the United States

Questions 9–11 are based on the following passage.

The work which Jurgis was to do here was very simple, and it took him but a few minutes to learn it. He was provided with a stiff besom, such as is used by street sweepers, and it was his place to follow down the line the man who drew out the smoking entrails from the carcass of the steer; this mass was to be swept into a trap, which was then closed, so that no one might slip into it. As Jurgis came in, the first cattle of the morning were just making their appearance, and so, with scarcely time to look about him, and none to speak to anyone, he fell to work. It was a sweltering day in July, and the place ran with steaming hot blood—one waded in it on the floor. The stench was almost overpowering, but to Jurgis it was nothing. His whole soul was dancing with joy—he was at work at last! He was at work and earning money! All day long he was figuring to himself. He was paid the fabulous sum of seventeen and a half cents an hour, and as it proved a rush day and he worked until nearly seven o'clock in the evening, he went home to the family with the tidings that he had earned more than a dollar and a half in a single day!

9. What is Jurgis employed as?

   (1) a worker in a slaughterhouse
   (2) a street sweeper
   (3) a hand on a ranch
   (4) a veterinarian's assistant
   (5) a skilled technician in a laboratory

10. Which of the following facts does the passage support?

   (1) Jurgis is not a hard and cooperative worker.
   (2) Jurgis obtained the job through a friend.
   (3) Jurgis needed special training for the job.
   (4) Jurgis had been unemployed for a long time.
   (5) Jurgis works alone, never seeing the other workers.

11. Jurgis is employed in the United States. In approximately what year is this story set?

   (1) 1905
   (2) 1945
   (3) 1960
   (4) 1970
   (5) 1995

Questions 12–14 are based on the information given about the following progressive reforms of the early twentieth century.

   Sherman Anti-Trust Act—outlawed monopolies, including price fixing and market sharing

   Hepburn Act—gave the Interstate Commerce Commission increased authority to regulate the nation's railroads

   Pure Food and Drug Act—set standards for the production and sale of food and drugs

   Child Labor Laws—put restrictions on the use of children in nonagricultural industries

   U.S. Department of Agriculture—inspected meat and other foods to protect the public's health

12. What principle did all these reforms abandon completely?

   (1) caveat emptor—"let the buyer beware" before making a purchase
   (2) laissez faire—a belief that government should not interfere with business
   (3) habeas corpus—the requirement to bring an accused person to court to face charges
   (4) social Darwinism—the belief that the wealthy and powerful are successful because of their biological superiority
   (5) diminishing returns—the return on investment fails to increase in relation to additional investment

13. Which of the reforms established guidelines for testing products for the potential dangers of cancer-producing substances contained in them?

    (1) Sherman Anti-Trust Act
    (2) Hepburn Act
    (3) Pure Food and Drug Act
    (4) Child Labor Laws
    (5) U.S. Department of Agriculture

14. Which of the reforms prohibited the employment of a person under age fifteen who had received less than three months of schooling in the previous year?

    (1) Sherman Anti-Trust Act
    (2) Hepburn Act
    (3) Pure Food and Drug Act
    (4) Child Labor Laws
    (5) U.S. Department of Agriculture

15. A weakness of the sales tax is that low-income persons pay a higher percentage of their income in taxes than do wealthy persons. Which of the following types of taxes would help reduce this unfair aspect of the retail sales tax?

    (1) an excise tax on alcoholic beverages sold in bottles or cans
    (2) a luxury tax on expensive jewelry and other costly items
    (3) an excise tax on cigarettes and tobacco products
    (4) a tax on gasoline and diesel fuel for cars and trucks
    (5) an excise tax on utilities such as electricity and water

16. A sales tax on which of the following items would be considered least unfair to the poor?

    (1) heating oil
    (2) clothing
    (3) food
    (4) cigarettes
    (5) electricity

Question 17 is based on the following graphic.

MASLOW'S HIERARCHY OF HUMAN NEEDS

Before you can experience love, you must feel safe, secure, and nourished. So says psychologist Abraham Maslow in his theory of a succeeding level of needs, shown in the chart above.

17. In general, in the United States, more affluent communities have higher rates of voter registration and voting than the poorest communities. Which hypothesis appears to be the best explanation of this phenomenon?

    (1) Poorer people are more interested in scandal and sensationalism than politics and elections.
    (2) Wealthier communities are more likely to have a high percentage of people with high self-esteem.
    (3) Politicians are not doing a good job of appealing to the needs of poor people and their communities.
    (4) Affluent communities depend on politicians to satisfy the communities' safety and security needs.
    (5) Poor people must devote more energy to day-to-day living, which does not include voting.

Questions 18 and 19 are based on the following passage.

Nearly 75 percent of the world's surface is water, yet it is the most critically short of all the natural resources. It is vital to human survival, each one of us requiring at least two or three quarts per day. Some of us, however, use more than fifty gallons a day. The misuse and overuse of water in some parts of the world, the difficulty in transporting the resource from water-rich areas to arid spots, and the pollution of many fresh water sources have all contributed to the irreversible shortage.

18. Which of the following statements is an opinion expressed or implied in the passage above?

   (1) Nearly 75 percent of the world's surface is covered by water.
   (2) There exists a severe water shortage throughout the world.
   (3) One person's use of fifty gallons of water per day constitutes misuse.
   (4) It is difficult to transport water across great distances.
   (5) The pollution of many fresh water sources has contributed to the shortage.

19. A *paradox* is a statement that is seemingly contradictory or opposed to common sense yet is true. What paradox is evident in the passage above?

   (1) People misuse and waste water even though they depend on it.
   (2) Most of the Earth's surface is water, but a shortage exists.
   (3) People can live off less than three quarts of water per day.
   (4) Many fresh water sources are polluted by human activity.
   (5) Some areas are water-rich while other areas are arid.

Questions 20–23 are based on the following terms.

pure capitalism—an economic system based on the private ownership of property and freedom of choice for consumers, with little or no governmental intervention

authoritarian socialism—an economic and social system in which private property is not permitted and the government subordinates individual choice to state-determined goals

liberal socialism—an economic system under which a country's major industries and services are owned both publicly and cooperatively and some governmental planning determines goals

manorial feudalism—an economic and social system in which one class of people provides protection and shelter for a lower class that pledges it loyalty and service

mercantilism—an economic system advocating commercial dominance over other nations, a buildup of gold reserves, a favorable balance of trade, and agricultural and industrial development

20. The economies of communist Vietnam, North Korea, and Cuba, in which goods are owned in common and private property is eliminated, are based on a system most similar to which of the following systems?

   (1) pure capitalism
   (2) authoritarian socialism
   (3) liberal socialism
   (4) manorial feudalism
   (5) mercantilism

21. The practice of imposing tariffs on imported goods in order to encourage the purchase of domestically manufactured goods originated under which of the following economic systems?

    (1) pure capitalism
    (2) authoritarian socialism
    (3) liberal socialism
    (4) manorial feudalism
    (5) mercantilism

22. A laissez-faire economy is characterized by competition among producers without governmental intervention. What is another name for this economic system?

    (1) pure capitalism
    (2) authoritarian socialism
    (3) liberal socialism
    (4) manorial feudalism
    (5) mercantilism

23. In the sharecropping system of the South, tenant farmers were provided credit for seed, tools, and living quarters. They worked the owner's land and agreed to share the crop's value with the owner. Which of the following systems is this similar to?

    (1) pure capitalism
    (2) authoritarian socialism
    (3) liberal socialism
    (4) manorial feudalism
    (5) mercantilism

24. During times of rapid inflation, loss of real income can occur if wages do not increase at the same rate as prices. Which of the following is a popular demand made by labor unions to correct this imbalance?

    (1) good medical and education benefits
    (2) shorter work weeks
    (3) seniority rights during lay-offs
    (4) cost-of-living adjustments
    (5) automatic predetermined raises

25. A major feature of a recession or a depression is high unemployment. A typical indicator of a healthy GNP (gross national product) is high employment. Therefore, what can we conclude would happen to the GNP during a recession or depression?

    It would
    (1) decrease
    (2) increase
    (3) fluctuate
    (4) be unaffected
    (5) be wiped out

Question 26 is based on the following chart.

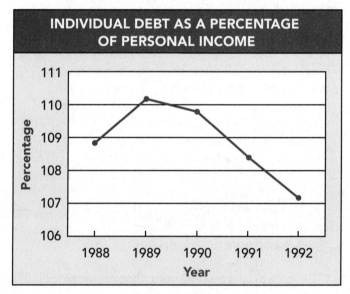

26. According to the information in this graph, what was the relationship between individual debt and personal income during the five-year period shown?

    (1) Individual debt always exceeded personal income.
    (2) Individual debt increased in proportion to personal income.
    (3) Individual debt and personal income held steady throughout.
    (4) Individual debt and personal income fluctuated together.
    (5) Individual debt forced a lowering of personal income.

Questions 27 and 28 are based on the following passage.

The Federal Reserve System (Fed) was created to prevent a recurrence of the collapse of the banking system and subsequent depression in the United States that occurred after the stock market crash of 1929. The system is made up of district banks located in twelve regions of the country. Through these banks (which are also clearinghouses in the check-clearing process), the Fed regulates the nation's money and credit supplies. Two ways by which the Fed does this are setting the reserve requirement and determining the discount rate. The reserve requirement is the percentage of deposits that banks must earmark as nonlendable. Therefore, it directly limits the amount of money that banks are allowed to lend to their customers. The discount rate is the interest rate that district banks charge member banks for borrowing. The discount rate indirectly sets the interest rate that consumers will pay for their loans.

27. What action would the Fed take if it wanted to decrease the money supply during a period of inflation?

(1) decrease the reserve requirement for member banks
(2) demand that the banks hold more money in reserve
(3) decrease the discount rate to its member banks
(4) decrease the commercial loan rate to the public
(5) free the banks to determine their own reserve ratio

28. If the Federal Reserve System were to charge its member banks a discount rate of 10 percent, which of the following would be the most likely rate charged on commercial loans?

(1) 4 percent
(2) 6 percent
(3) 8 percent
(4) 10 percent
(5) 12 percent

29. In their first year on the market in Japan, DAT (digital audiotape) recorders received much positive publicity, but they did not sell well. What best explains the surprisingly low success of a much-heralded technological improvement?

(1) the trade imbalance between Japan and the United States
(2) the high inflation rate in effect in Japan at the time
(3) the lowering of prices on the machines and their tapes
(4) the small number of prerecorded DAT tapes on the market
(5) the large number of DAT recorders flooding the market

30. The sluggish sales of Japan's DATs is most similar to which of the following situations that occurred in the consumer electronics industry?

(1) Japan's domination of the consumer electronics industry
(2) the entrance of Korean manufacturers into the industry
(3) the phasing out of Sony's beta-formatted videocassette recorder
(4) the ongoing popularity of VHS-compatible VCRs
(5) the imposition of quotas on all Japanese imports to the United States

Questions 31 and 32 are based on the following passage.

The economic growth of a country is measured by the amount of goods and services it produces over a given period of time. The degree of growth depends on a certain combination of characteristics. For optimum growth, these characteristics would include the following:

- an abundance of high quality natural resources

- natural and human-made resources used to full capacity

- the ability and willingness to invest in capital goods

- a labor force capable of growing in size and quality

- a constant increase in aggregate demand (total spending)

31. Northern Essex Community College gives intensive training to its computer faculty in the latest computer-repair technology so they can retrain local workers displaced from their jobs. The college is contributing to which factor in economic growth?

    (1) an abundance of natural resources
    (2) full use of available resources
    (3) investment in capital goods
    (4) a growing, trainable labor force
    (5) an increase in aggregate demand

32. During a recession consumers usually spend less money, putting off purchases until better economic times return. This behavior directly affects which factor related to economic growth?

    (1) an abundance of natural resources
    (2) full use of available resources
    (3) investment in capital goods
    (4) a growing, trainable labor force
    (5) an increase in aggregate demand

Questions 33–35 are based on the following terms.

sole proprietorship—a business owned and managed by one person

partnership—an agreement between two or more persons to own and operate a business together

limited partnership—a partnership in which liability for business debts is limited to the amount of money each partner has invested in the business

corporation—a business organization recognized by law to act as a legal person with rights and privileges and whose individual owners are not personally liable for its debts

cooperative—a business enterprise whose owners are its own customers and whose purpose is usually to save money on purchases

33. A group of neighbors and friends who get together to form a business to buy grocery products at wholesale prices may by described as which of the following?

    (1) sole proprietorship
    (2) partnership
    (3) limited partnership
    (4) corporation
    (5) cooperative

34. For which type of business is a single business owner entirely responsible for all business debts?

    (1) sole proprietorship
    (2) partnership
    (3) limited partnership
    (4) corporation
    (5) cooperative

35. What is one similarity between a limited partnership and a corporation?

The owners
(1) are treated as customers in the business
(2) share equally in business decisions
(3) share equally in the business's profits
(4) have limited or no liability for business debts
(5) have personal liability for all business debts

Questions 36–38 are based on the following graph.

U.S. CONSUMER PRICES

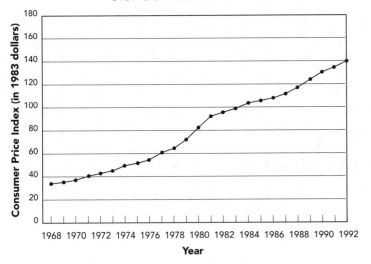

36. Between August 1971 and April 1974, the federal government attempted to control a fast-rising Consumer Price Index (CPI) by instituting a series of programs such as price and wage controls. According to the graph, what was the effect of these programs?

(1) They managed to reverse inflation.
(2) They helped to hold prices steady.
(3) They were mostly ineffective.
(4) They had a long-lasting effect.
(5) They reduced economic growth.

37. In 2000 the CPI was 172. This information proves which of the following?

(1) The CPI data in this chart is misleading.
(2) Inflation was still a major problem in 2000.
(3) The rate of inflation slowed after 1992.
(4) This chart was an accurate predictor of future inflation.
(5) The economy must have slowed down in the 1990s.

38. This CPI is a gauge for measuring a rise in prices, or inflation, from year to year by using 1983 prices as a standard. For example, a shopping cart full of groceries that cost $100 in 1983 might cost about $140 in 1992. Based on this definition, what does the CPI measure?

(1) economic growth
(2) cost of living
(3) supply and demand
(4) balance of trade
(5) gross national product

Questions 39–41 are based on the following passage.

Although only 14 percent of the businesses in the United States are corporations, they account for roughly 85 percent of the business transacted. Corporations are owned by stockholders or shareholders who purchase stock or shares in the organization. Stockholders can vote for the corporation's board of directors. One vote is given for each share of common stock owned, so the more stock owned, the more influence wielded.

One advantage of a corporation is that it can raise money for capital investments and improvements by selling bonds as well as by offering additional shares of stock. Bonds are certificates bought by investors that are repaid at a guaranteed rate of interest on a designated maturity date. On the other hand, stockholders earn dividends for the money they invest. Dividends are not guaranteed, however, and are usually paid only when the corporation's profits permit it.

39. What is one big difference between owning common stock and owning bonds from a corporation?

   (1) Stockholders get a guaranteed return on their investment; bond owners do not.
   (2) Stockholders get their returns by specified dates each year; bond owners do not.
   (3) Stockholders help a corporation improve itself financially; bond owners do not.
   (4) Stockholders vote for those who control the company; bond owners do not.
   (5) Stockholders appoint the officers of a corporation; bond owners do not.

40. Preferred stock is guaranteed priority over common stock in the payment of dividends and in the distribution of assets. If a corporation is forced to dissolve and must pay all of its creditors interest and dividends, which would be the proper order in which to pay the claimants?

   (1) preferred stockholders, common stockholders, bond owners
   (2) common stockholders, preferred stockholders, bond owners
   (3) bond owners, common stockholders, preferred stockholders
   (4) bond owners, preferred stockholders, common stockholders
   (5) common stockholders, bond owners, preferred stockholders

41. The laws for chartering corporations vary from state to state and contain provisions that may protect either the individual private investor or the organizers of the corporation. Most states favor the interests of the individual investor over the organizers (management). A corporation that is chartered in its own state is called a *domestic corporation*. One that is chartered in another state (or nation) is called a *foreign corporation*. The small state of Delaware is home to numerous corporations and is nicknamed the "Corporation State." Based on the facts above, you can infer that Delaware is home to more foreign corporations than any other state for what reason?

   (1) It does not regulate corporations in any way or require them to pay any taxes at all to the state.
   (2) It has corporation laws more favorable to management's interests than to individual investors' interests.
   (3) It has corporation laws more favorable to individual investors' interests than to management's interests.
   (4) It has fair and equitable laws that favor neither individual investors nor management.
   (5) It actively seeks the business of corporations through aggressive, nationwide advertising campaigns.

Questions 42 and 43 are based on the following chart.

Douglas Aircraft Co., Selected Statistics, 1939–1944

Year	Revenue Income (millions of dollars)		Earnings Dividends (per share)		Price Range Common Stock High Low	
1939	28.0	2.9	$4.81	$3.00	87 3/4	55
1940	61.1	10.8	18.05	5.00	94 7/8	65 1/8
1941	181.4	18.2	30.29	5.00	79 1/4	59 1/4
1942	501.8	11.1	15.38	5.00	70 3/4	51
1943	987.7	6.0	9.92	5.00	72 1/2	47

Source: *Moody's Manual, 1942, 1945*

42. From the facts in the table, what can you infer was the single most important factor in the dramatic rise of the aircraft industry during the period shown?

(1) the beginning of the Great Depression in the United States
(2) the entry of the United States into World War II
(3) the growing strength of labor unions around the world
(4) the increase of leisure time for Americans
(5) the rapid decline of the railroad industry

43. In the chart, the company's revenues increased every year between 1939 and 1943, but the income (profit) did not. Which of the following is the most probable explanation for this?

(1) The stock price decreased after 1941.
(2) The top officials in the company were embezzling funds.
(3) The company was investing more in labor and other resources.
(4) The demand for aircraft decreased after 1941.
(5) Many workers were laid off in 1942 and 1943.

44. The owners of the Watch Video Store went into business when they found that no other video store existed within a five-mile radius of their store's location, and many families in the area owned video players. What economic factor prompted the owners to open their store?

(1) supply
(2) demand
(3) surplus
(4) equilibrium
(5) barter

Questions 45 and 46 are based on the following cartoon.

ANOTHER ADDICTIVE ELEMENT THEY DON'T LIKE TO TALK ABOUT...

Questions 47 and 48 are based on the following cartoon.

45. What is the main point the cartoonist is making?

  (1) The tobacco industry depends on government subsidies.
  (2) Smoking is an extremely unattractive habit.
  (3) The tobacco industry has too much power over Congress.
  (4) The tobacco industry is weak and vulnerable.
  (5) The tobacco industry is secretive and dishonest.

46. From the cartoon, what can you infer about the tobacco industry?

  (1) It is thriving because of the desirability of its product.
  (2) It is threatened by increased government regulation.
  (3) It is trying to survive by attracting new customers.
  (4) It recently started receiving government aid.
  (5) It has been slow to admit that nicotine is addictive.

47. What is the main point of this cartoon?

  (1) Government claims that the economy is improving are false.
  (2) The restaurant industry is not participating in the recent boom.
  (3) The new jobs created in America are not going to women.
  (4) Recent gains in the economy have not benefited all workers.
  (5) American service workers complain too much.

48. Which of the following is probably the most important reason the artist uses a waitress as an example in this cartoon?

  (1) Many of the new jobs being created are low-paying service positions such as waiting on tables.
  (2) He wants to make men more aware of the economic pressures put on working women.
  (3) Waitresses tend to be willing to talk more about the economy than other people.
  (4) The food industry has been one of the slowest to recover from the recession.
  (5) Waitresses are involved in business, so they are in touch with business trends.

Question 49 is based on the following passage.

The media called October 19, 1987, "Black Monday." On that day, the stock market nearly collapsed, plunging over 500 points. Many experts blamed it all on a handful of aggressive young investors who devised a computerized scheme that would provide protection against falling prices.

49. According to the passage, what do many experts think was the cause of Black Monday?

   (1) the media's exploitation of stock market uncertainty
   (2) fighting among the stock market investors
   (3) a strategy pursued by inexperienced speculators
   (4) the refusal of a few investors to share their secrets
   (5) the failure of the computers to predict the crash

Question 50 is based on the following chart.

50. According to the evidence in the chart, what happened from March 2000 to March 2001 to the total value of publicly owned companies headquartered in the United States?

   (1) Publicly owned companies lost almost all of their value.
   (2) Publicly owned companies rebounded after a period of panic.
   (3) Publicly owned companies lost more than 20% of their value.
   (4) The value of publicly owned companies returned to a reasonable level.
   (5) Publicly owned companies were valued at far less than their true worth.

Answers are on pages 142–144.

Go to **www.GEDSocialStudies.com** for additional practice and instruction!

Chapter 5

Science, Technology, and Society

GED Social Studies pages 253–282
Complete GED pages 420–426

Questions 1 and 2 refer to the following graph.

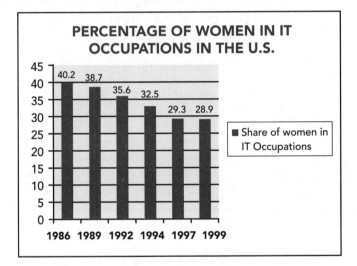

PERCENTAGE OF WOMEN IN IT OCCUPATIONS IN THE U.S.

40.2 38.7 35.6 32.5 29.3 28.9

1986 1989 1992 1994 1997 1999

■ Share of women in IT Occupations

"IT" refers to "Information Technology," and is generally associated with computers.

1. Who among the following is represented by the information in the graph?

   (1) a sixteen-year-old girl who becomes discouraged in her computer class in 1992 and quits studying computers
   (2) a corporate executive who hires a large number of women for his technology company in 1986
   (3) a recent GED recipient who decides to pursue nursing instead of computer science in 1997
   (4) a female software engineer who leaves her job in an IT company and becomes a science teacher in 1999
   (5) a group of men in a technology company who conspire to harass a woman until she quits her job

2. Which of the following statements is the least likely explanation of the trend illustrated in the graph?

   (1) In the 1990s women may not have experienced as much support and encouragement to enter IT. occupations as they had previously.
   (2) In the 1990s the competitive climate in many technology companies was comfortable for more men than women.
   (3) In the 1990s fewer women graduated from technology or engineering programs at colleges and universities than in past years.
   (4) In the 1990s many technology companies decided they didn't want female employees and openly discriminated against female applicants.
   (5) In the 1990s jobs in technology were stereotyped as being more suited to males than females and women turned away from them.

69

Questions 3 and 4 refer to the following passage.

The ziggurats of Mesopotamia and the pyramids of Egypt symbolize the organizational power and the technological magnitude of the first urban settlements. The pyramid of Kind Djoser, who reigned in Egypt from 2630–2611 B.C.E., was built at Saqqarah by Imhotep around 2620 B.C.E. The first engineer known by name, Imhotep was worshiped as one of the gods of wisdom. The Great Pyramid of King Khufu involved the organization of more than 100,000 workers and the cutting of 2.3 million blocks of stone, each weighing 2 to 4 metric tons. The construction of such massive buildings and monuments, the growth of trade in metalware, and the development of water-resource management also brought about a standardization of measurement. In Mesopotamia the cubit became the standard of length, and the shekel the standard of weight. Time was measured in Egypt with a calendar that divided the yearly cycle of seasons into months and days.

3. From the passage, you can infer that a *ziggurat* is similar to which of the following?

    (1) a book
    (2) a calendar
    (3) a pyramid
    (4) an aqueduct
    (5) a mine

4. The passage tells us that the ancient civilizations of Mesopotamia and Egypt were responsible for all except which of the following?

    (1) starting slavery
    (2) large-scale construction
    (3) ways to control water use and availability
    (4) a system for weight and measurement
    (5) a means of marking time

Questions 5 and 6 are based on the following passage and graph.

In 1992, when the last Chilean census was taken, 240,000 homes in the country did not have electricity. During the last few years, several different systems have been implemented in rural areas to generate power: small hydraulic plants in southern Chile to take advantage of a greater hydraulic capacity, and Solar Home Systems (SHS) in northern Chile where there is more solar radiation. The Solar Home System consists of one photovoltaic panel, a charge regulator, one battery, lights, one socket, and switches. In 2000 a survey was conducted of the people in whose homes the SHS had been installed. Some of the results of the survey are reported in the graph below.

—Adapted from "Introducing Photovoltaic Systems into Homes in Rural Chile," www.njcc.com/~techsoc/cancino.html

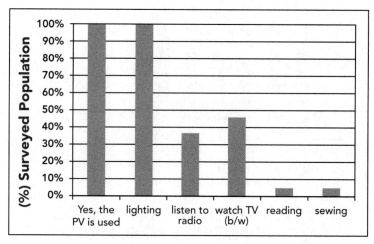

—from "Introducing Photovoltaic Systems into Homes in Rural Chile" by Beatriz Cancino, et. al as appeared on www.njcc.com ©2001 IEEE. Reprinted by permission.

5. Which of the following criteria was *least* critical in deciding the means of bringing electricity to rural Chile?

    (1) extremely powerful
    (2) easily transported
    (3) easily repaired
    (4) low cost
    (5) taps natural energy sources

6. On the basis of the information presented here, what generalization might you be tempted to make about the people in rural Chile?

   (1) Almost every household in rural Chile has a television set.
   (2) Radio is the preferred form of home entertainment in rural Chile.
   (3) Most people in rural Chile wear clothing made at home.
   (4) Only a few people know how to read or choose to read at night.
   (5) There is a small percentage of people who don't want electric lights.

Questions 7–9 are based on the following passage.

The Soviet program gave off an aura of sorcery. The Soviets released practically no figures, pictures, or diagrams. And no names; it was revealed only that the Soviet program was guided by a mysterious individual known as "The Chief Designer." But his powers were indisputable! Every time the United States announced a great space experiment, the Chief Designer accomplished it first, in the most startling fashion. In 1955 the United States announced plans to launch an artificial earth satellite by early 1958. The Chief Designer startles the world by doing it in October 1957. The United States announces plans to send a satellite into orbit around the sun in March of 1959. The Chief Designer does it in January 1959. The fact that the United States went ahead and successfully conducted such experiments on schedule, as announced, impressed no one—and Americans least of all.

—Excerpted from *The Right Stuff* by Tom Wolfe

7. Why weren't Americans impressed by the United States' accomplishments in the space program in the 1950s?

   Because the United States
   (1) was always behind in the schedule it had set
   (2) always accomplished its goals after the Soviets had
   (3) would not cooperate with the Soviet Chief Designer
   (4) engineers did not have the same resources as the Chief Designer
   (5) engineers did not make their plans as well known as the Soviets did

8. Which of the following characteristics did the American public of the 1950s value most highly during the progress of the space programs?

   (1) patriotism
   (2) carefulness
   (3) swiftness
   (4) materialism
   (5) mysteriousness

9. Which of the following is a logical conclusion, based on the information given in the passage?

   (1) If the Chief Designer had revealed his plans to the world, the United States might have made faster progress in its space program.
   (2) If the Chief Designer had worked for the United States, America might have accomplished its space program advancements earlier.
   (3) If the Chief Designer had not beat the United States' deadlines, the Americans might not have met them on time.
   (4) If the Chief Designer had worked for any country other than the Soviet Union, he might not have been so successful.
   (5) If the United States had found a way to put someone on the moon in July 1959, the Soviets would probably have done it by May 1959.

Question 10 is based on the following photograph.

10. Who would have been most likely to use this photograph to support their cause?

(1) an advertiser promoting the newest labor-saving device for the home
(2) a textile company that wants to emphasize the high quality of its fabric
(3) an activist concerned about the health and education of child workers
(4) an environmentalist protesting the negative effects of production on rivers
(5) the author of the operating manual for the machine shown in the picture

Questions 11–13 refer to the following passage.

The Anglo-Saxon identified elves as the Devil's particular lieutenants in the mortification of the body. People spoke of "elf-shot" as we today would talk of germs, explaining infection as something that had been caused by an invisible arrow or dart fired off by some malevolent sprite—and the logic of that was that an arrow should feature in the cure. If you suffered from a stitch in your side or from a particularly bad pain, one tenth-century German remedy recommended placing an arrowhead or some other piece of metal on the sore spot, and then uttering this charm: "Come out, worm, with nine little worms, out from the marrow into the bone, from the bone into the flesh, from the flesh into the skin, from the skin into this arrow." And just in case this invocation sounded pagan, the sufferer was told to add the prayer: "So be it, Lord."

—Excerpted from *The Year 1000: What Life Was Like at the Turn of the First Millennium* by Robert Lacey and Danny Danzinger

11. From the passage it is clear that Anglo-Saxons in the 10th century did not yet understand the relationship between which of the following?

(1) paganism and Christianity
(2) elves and arrows
(3) pain and infection
(4) flesh and skin
(5) germs and infection

12. Which of the following medical developments has replaced the arrow cure?

(1) exorcism
(2) anesthesia
(3) skin grafting
(4) antibiotics
(5) x-rays

13. What can be concluded from the passage about Anglo-Saxon society in the 10th century?

(1) People's imaginations controlled every aspect of their lives.
(2) The Judeo-Christian belief system had started to replace the pagan one.
(3) Magic was the most common way of dealing with disease and misfortune.
(4) The field of medicine was making stunning advances.
(5) German was becoming the dominant language in Europe.

Questions 14 and 15 refer to the following passage and chart.

The development of vaccines by modern medicine has dramatically reduced the incidence of a number of deadly diseases. A vaccine triggers the body's immune system to build a defense mechanism that continuously guards against a disease. Below is the schedule of immunizations that was recommended for children in the United States in 2000.

RECOMMENDED CHILDHOOD IMMUNIZATION SCHEDULE — UNITED STATES, JANUARY–DECEMBER 2000

Vaccine	Birth	1 mo	2 mo	4 mo	6 mo	12 mo	15 mo	18 mo	24 mo	4-6 yrs	11-12 yrs	12-16 yrs
Hepatitis B	Hep B	Hep B			Hep B						Hep B	
Diptheria and tetanus toxoids and pertussis			DTaP	DTaP	DTaP		DTaP			DTaP	Td	
H. Influenzae type b			Hib	Hib	Hib	Hib						
Polio			IPV	IPV	IPV					IPV		
Measles - mumps - rubella					MMR					MMR	MMR	
Varicella					Var						Var	
Hepatitis A									Hep A selected areas			

☐ Range of recommended ages for vaccination.

⬭ Vaccines to be given if previously recommended doses were missed or were given earlier than the recommended minimum age.

▨ Recommended in selected states and/or regions.

14. What does the chart reveal about childhood immunizations?

(1) To be immunized as suggested requires regular visits to a doctor.
(2) The first of the vaccines to be developed was that for polio.
(3) There is a vaccine available for every deadly disease.
(4) All children in the United States received these vaccines in 2001.
(5) All children should be immunized against Hepatitis A in their first year.

15. Which of the following statements is likely to be true about immunization?

(1) All children in the world are immunized according to a schedule similar to one on the chart.
(2) It is a good idea for children to be immunized between the ages of five and ten.
(3) The diseases for which there are now vaccines were never much of a threat until recently.
(4) In countries with a lower standard of living than that of the United States, fewer children are immunized.
(5) Immunizations are extremely painful for infants and young children and have some serious side effects.

Questions 16 and 17 refer to the follo

16. All of the frames of this cartoon imply that history might have been different if today's information technology had been available. Which of the following episodes in history that are depicted here had the *least* impact upon the future, regardless of whether the handheld computer was available?

(1) Christopher Columbus's journey to the New World
(2) George Washington's dental needs
(3) the sinking of the *Titanic*
(4) the bombing of Pearl Harbor
(5) the assassination of John Kennedy

17. What was the artist's purpose in creating this caroon?

(1) to demonstrate that the handheld computer has had a long and interesting history
(2) to assert that all of history would have been different had there been handheld computers
(3) to explain that a handheld computer can perform many diverse and remarkable functions
(4) to suggest that handheld computers could have had an impact on only a few historical events
(5) to illustrate that a handheld computer might have influenced the outcome of some events in American history

Questions 18–21 refer to the following passage.

Historically, technology has had a huge impact on the use of language. Around 1811, the steam engine collided with the printing press, and the result was as explosive then as the collision of computers with the telephone network is now. The rotary-driven steam press printed hundreds of times faster than any other available technology—so fast that publishers couldn't afford to feed enough paper into those voracious machines. In the 1850s, some clever Germans invented a cheap pulp papermaking process. The new stuff became known as newsprint, since that's largely what it was used for, and with the force of this flow, the modern newspaper took shape.

Soon it became clear that paper was no longer the scarce resource. Nor were printing presses, or even news. The scarce resource? Readers. In 1858, only one in 20 British army recruits could read. Other European societies had similar levels of literacy. And so, in countries across Europe, as well as in America, policymakers began mandating more systematic schooling. By 1900, literacy among British recruits had jumped to more than 85 percent and the novel had become a mainstream art form. Mass public literacy, therefore, was an outgrowth of a burst of technology that liberated a huge quantity of text, and then encouraged an ensuing ballet of sorts among policymakers, educators, authors and printers.

—Excerpted from "Waiting for Linguistic Viagra" by Michael Hawley, *Technology* Review, June 2001

18. The passage refers to all except which of the following?

(1) the development of the newspaper
(2) the design of the original printing press
(3) a reason for mandated schooling
(4) the similarity between the Internet and mass printing
(5) the impact of inventions on public policy

19. Which of the following explanations is given in the passage for governments requiring school for children?

(1) There was much to read but few to read it.
(2) Only army officers knew how to read.
(3) Too many people were waiting for computers.
(4) There was a great demand for novels and newspapers.
(5) The Germans insisted that school was necessary.

20. The pairing of the steam engine with the printing press was a part of which major social movement?

(1) women's liberation
(2) civil rights
(3) suburban sprawl
(4) the Industrial Revolution
(5) the Renaissance

21. Why does the author compare the combination of the steam engine and the printing press to that of the computer and the telephone?

(1) Each is a combination of a more recent and an older invention.
(2) Both happened around the same historical time period.
(3) Both caused swift and sweeping changes to society.
(4) Both caused an increase in literacy rates.
(5) Both involved an increase in the amount of paper used.

Questions 22 and 23 are based on passage below.

Along the coast of the Gulf of Mexico early inhabitants lived mainly on what they could catch from the sea and practiced ceremonial cannibalism. They made pottery that was waterproofed with asphalt. In central Texas large refuse piles built up over many years have shown that there were advances in technology during the Stone Age. More advanced stone implements were found in the top layers of the refuse than at the bottom. Dwellings made of stone slabs were discovered along the Canadian River in the Texas Panhandle. The people who lived there hunted and planted corn and beans. An early people, whom archaeologists call Basket Makers, settled in the Texas Panhandle and along the Pecos River. They lived in caves or built shelters of poles and adobe mud. They made baskets, bags, and sandals from the yucca and other plants and raised corn and squash and killed game with a dart thrower.

22. The information in this passage supports which of the following facts about early human settlement?

(1) Humans have almost always built their shelters out of stone.
(2) Stone tools were all that early humans crafted from their environment.
(3) Humans frequently settled along rivers or other sources of water.
(4) An agricultural way of life preceded one of constant wandering.
(5) Texas is the site of the earliest remains of human activity.

23. All except which of the following findings in Texas were evidence of technological development?

(1) waterproof pottery
(2) ceremonial cannibalism
(3) stone implements
(4) corn, bean, and squash gardens
(5) baskets, bags, and sandals

Questions 24 and 25 refer to the following cartoon.

24. What is the likely response of the couple in the cartoon to the pollster?

(1) We don't use the Net because we don't have enough money for a computer.
(2) We use the Net frequently because we have a lot of spare time.
(3) We use the Net frequently because it is important for our job.
(4) We use the Net only when we want to trade on the stock market.
(5) We don't use the Net because we consider it outdated.

25. Which of the following elements makes this cartoon humorous?

(1) Most Latinos do not like to use computers.
(2) Migrant farm workers probably wouldn't wear nets.
(3) The farm workers are speaking in English rather than in Spanish.
(4) The farm workers probably do not know what the Internet is.
(5) Pollsters do not usually do their polling on farms.

Questions 26 and 27 refer to the graph below.

PRACTICE AND SPEED IN CIGAR-MAKING

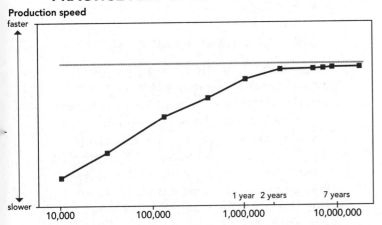

26. For whom would the information in this graph be most supportive, and therefore, most valuable?

    (1) an aging worker whose quality of product remains high but at the expense of quantity
    (2) a company president who wants to hire new workers for his factory assembly lines
    (3) members of the antismoking lobby who are pressuring for stricter controls on cigar production.
    (4) a company manager in favor of keeping more experienced workers instead of hiring new ones
    (5) the inventor of a new machine that is not yet able to replicate the speed of human workers

27. According to the graph what is the advantage of machines in industry?

    (1) A machine never operates any faster or more efficiently.
    (2) Machines give more people jobs and thus keep the economy healthy.
    (3) A machine starts at and maintains a high level of production.
    (4) Machines are much less expensive to maintain than people.
    (5) Machines are always being improved but people are not.

Questions 28 and 29 refer to the following passage.

Telecommunications technologies—computers, satellites, interactive television, telephone, and radio—are breaking down the age-old barriers of time and distance that originally precluded the nation's people from voting directly for the laws and policies that govern them. The general belief holds that representative government is the only form of democracy that is feasible in today's sprawling heterogeneous nation-states. However, interactive telecommunication now makes it possible for tens of millions of widely dispersed citizens to receive the information they need to carry out the business of government themselves, gain admission to the political realm, and retrieve at least some of the power over their own lives and goods that many believe their elected leaders are squandering.

—Excerpted from "The Electronic Republic" by Lawrence K. Grossman, *Perspectives: Readings on Contemporary American Government*

28. From this passage, what can one infer about representative democracy?

    (1) It is not a legitimate form of government.
    (2) It forbids the use of telecommunications.
    (3) It is currently a common form of government.
    (4) It always leads to corruption among leaders.
    (5) It has supported the growth of telecommunications.

29. What would the author of this passage be most likely to do?

    (1) support citizens who want a role in directly deciding government policy with the use of telecommunication technologies
    (2) protest the use of public funding to give more American citizens access to telecommunications technology
    (3) vote for politicians who have been accused of taking bribes to support legislation that will benefit special-interest groups
    (4) campaign for a simpler lifestyle in America that is not so dependent upon computers, television, and telephones
    (5) criticize telecommunication manufacturers for introducing new products before the public is ready for them

Questions 30 and 31 refer to the following article from the People's Journal of London on January 9, 1847. It refers to the discovery and successful use of ether as an anesthetic in surgery.

THE GOOD NEWS FROM AMERICA

Hail happy hour! That brings the glad tidings of another glorious victory. Oh, what delight for every feeling heart to find the new year ushered in with the announcement of this noble discovery of the power to still the sense of pain, and veil the eye and memory for all the horrors of an operation. And then to find it acted upon almost on the instant by our first operators, is as gratifying as unexpected. WE HAVE CONQUERED PAIN. This is indeed a glorious victory to announce; a victory of the pure intellect. And from America comes the happy news; from our brothers in another land, with whom we were lately going to war. Oh, shame be in the thought! This is indeed a glorious victory; but there is no blow struck, there has been no grappling together in the war of savage impulse, no bloodshed, no remorse. It is the victory of knowledge over ignorance, of good over evil: there is no alloy; all our finer sympathies are enlisted in one universal prayer of grateful rejoicing. Benevolence has its triumph. It is a victory not for to-day, nor for our own time, but for another age, and all time—not for one nation, but for all nations, from generation to generation, as long as the world shall last.

—Excerpted from the 1847 article, *We Have Conquered Pain: The Discovery of Anesthesia* by Dennis Brindell Fradin

 Go to **www.GEDSocialStudies.com** for additional practice and instruction!

30. What conviction does this article support?

   (1) that scientific discoveries should belong to and be protected by only the nation in which the discovery was made

   (2) that anesthesia should be used only in England since much of the United States used to be British colonies

   (3) that pain is necessary for strengthening the soul, and therefore, anesthesia is an evil that should be banned

   (4) that science recognizes no national boundaries and its benefits are for all, both now and in the future

   (5) that the discovery of anesthesia is a hoax that will soon be exposed to the public by investigative reporters in Britain

31. The discovery of anesthesia was most likely to have had an impact on those involved in which of the following historical events?

   (1) the American Revolution
   (2) the American Civil War
   (3) the Age of Exploration
   (4) the War of 1812
   (5) the founding of the British colonies

Questions 32 and 33 refer to the passage below.

On April 26, 1986, one of the nuclear reactors at the Chernobyl nuclear power plant in the Ukraine exploded, releasing toxic radiation into the atmosphere. Residents within a radius of approximately 20 miles of the plant were evacuated. In the weeks following the explosion, cleanup crews worked to contain the damage. However, much of the area surrounding the plant still contains high levels of radiation. The Chernobyl disaster was a tragic lesson in the importance of nuclear reactor safety.

32. The effects of the explosion at Chernobyl were most likely compared to that of which other phenomenon?

   (1) the San Francisco earthquake of 1989
   (2) the volcanic eruption of Mount Vesuvius in 79 C.E.
   (3) the bubonic plague in 14th century Cairo, Egypt
   (4) the drought in northeast and Central Africa in the 1980s
   (5) the fallout of the atomic bomb blasts in Japan in 1945

33. Which of the following would probably *not* have been affected by the Chernobyl explosion?

   (1) the cleaning-crew members
   (2) plants and animals in the woods near the plant
   (3) children in the town ten miles away
   (4) people working in the power plant
   (5) the water supply for nearby communities

Questions 34–36 refer to the passage below.

From a technological viewpoint, the Greeks and Romans could have produced an industrial revolution by utilizing the knowledge of steam, air pressure, and meshing gears, which was squandered on temple miracles and gadgets for the state. The recently recovered Antikythera computer dispels any doubt about ancient mechanical aptitude. Although they did not use fossil fuels, the Greeks were aware of Near Eastern oil fields, where some deposits had accidentally ignited and burned for years. Long before Eli Whitney, the Romans manufactured interchangeable parts for items to be assembled elsewhere. An orientation toward mass consumption would surely have encouraged industrial research and the development of new techniques and better metals and fuels. However, the agrarian population was desperately poor, and wealth was concentrated in the cities. While the buying capacity of the city bourgeoisie was large, their numbers were limited, and thus ancient society's purchasing power was too low to warrant mass production of non-necessities. Therefore, it can be said that the impetus for an industrial scientific complex was prevented by the social and economic structure. In the long run, poverty sabotaged the mechanization of the ancient world.

—Adapted from *Science and the State in Greece and Rome* by Thomas W. Africa

34. The information in this passage *contradicts* which of the following statements?

    (1) Economics is not only a factor in a society's technological development but the critical ingredient for determining how far that society will advance.
    (2) The human potential to develop the tools necessary for launching an industrial revolution has only existed for the last two hundred years.
    (3) If the Greeks and Romans had distributed their resources more equitably among their people, they would have had the means to progress technologically.
    (4) Inventions have often been made earlier in history than is recognized but, because of reasons unrelated to the inventions themselves, have not received wide public use.
    (5) The Greeks and Romans used technological expertise in what from today's perspective appears to be inconsequential and unnecessary ways.

35. According to the passage, which of the following would *not* have contributed to the potential technological progress of the ancient Greeks and Romans?

    (1) gas and oil
    (2) an early form of the computer
    (3) large scale manufacturing
    (4) antibiotics
    (5) copper and steel

36. Which part of today's world reflects most closely the socio-economic conditions of ancient Greece and Rome as described in the passage, resulting in a similar failure to progress technologically?

    (1) Japan
    (2) the west coast of the U.S.
    (3) northern Europe
    (4) Australia
    (5) sub-Saharan Africa

Questions 37 and 38 refer to the following two maps.

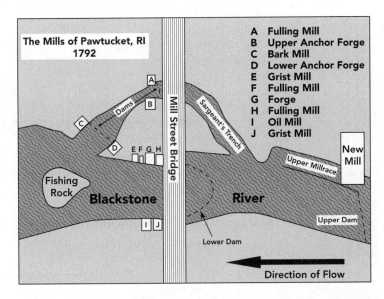

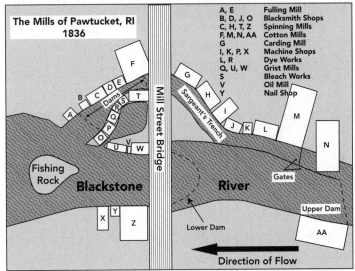

37. What *cannot* be inferred from the two maps about the changes in the Pawtucket area of the Blackstone River between 1792 and 1836?

(1) The river had begun to be polluted with refuse from the mills.
(2) More people worked along this portion of the river in 1836 than in 1792.
(3) Politicians were opposed to the increase of buildings along the river.
(4) More housing was being built in Pawtucket and neighboring towns in 1836 than in 1792.
(5) The economy of the area was based more heavily on the textile industry.

38. In what way was this area probably similar to other areas in which mills were being built in this time period?

(1) It was in Rhode Island.
(2) Its river flowed west.
(3) It was near a large city.
(4) People spoke the same language.
(5) It was on a river.

Questions 39—43 are based on the following diagram.

DIAGRAM OF EMERGING INSTITUTIONS IN CIVILIZED SOCIETY

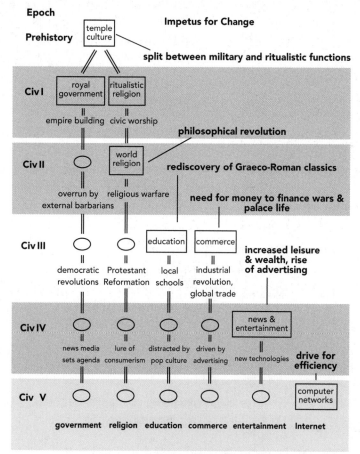

40. According to the diagram, which of the following is correct about the current epoch?

    (1) There are no new institutions.
    (2) An issue in education is consumerism.
    (3) Religion will soon cease to be an institution.
    (4) There are six main institutions.
    (5) It is completely disconnected from CivI.

41. In which epoch does the American Revolution fall?

    (1) CivI
    (2) CivII
    (3) CivIII
    (4) CivIV
    (5) CivV

42. In which epoch is the impact of technology greatest on the most institutions?

    (1) CivI
    (2) CivII
    (3) CivIII
    (4) CivIV
    (5) CivV

39. Each square on the diagram represents a significant institution of human society. What do the ovals represent?

    (1) a lack of change in institutions
    (2) smaller, less significant institutions
    (3) the continued presence of each institution
    (4) the number of centuries that each epoch lasted
    (5) each epoch's belief about the number of planets

43. It is evident from the diagram that the person who designed it takes which of the following views?

    (1) The Internet is not as important an institution as education.
    (2) There is no relationship between war and business.
    (3) Civilized society and its institutions will progress no further.
    (4) All human developments can be traced to a single source.
    (5) Religion is simply a matter of philosophy.

Questions 44 and 45 are based on the following passage.

A patent is a legal document granted by the government which gives the inventor the exclusive right to make, use, and sell his or her invention for a specified number of years. In the United States, patents last for 20 years. The goal of the patent system is to encourage inventors to advance the state of technology by giving them special rights which allow them to benefit from their inventions. Patent law is one branch of the larger legal field known as intellectual property, which also includes trademark and copyright law. Patent protection has great economic importance to a number of industries that rely on technological innovation to remain competitive, such as the chemical, pharmaceutical, and computer industries.

The U.S. government grants patents for machines; compositions of matter, such as new chemical compounds to be used in industry; manufactured items; and industrial processes, as long as they meet certain strict legal tests. Patents are also available for significant improvements on previously invented items. Special patents can be obtained for the invention or discovery and asexual reproduction of new types of vegetation. Patents may also be granted for certain types of industrial designs, such as a distinct tread pattern on the soles of hiking boots or tennis shoes. Computer programs have been granted patent protection, as have various living organisms, such as specialized mice that were bred to help in cancer research. Books, movies, and works of art cannot be patented, but protection is available for such items under copyright law.

To qualify for a patent, an invention must meet three basic tests. First, it must be "novel," meaning that it did not previously exist. If the patent examiner finds that the invention has already been described in previous patents or written about in scientific magazines, the examiner will declare that the invention has been "anticipated" and the patent will be denied. Second, the invention must be "non-obvious," which means that it

must be a significant improvement to existing technology. Simple changes to devices that already exist do not comprise a patentable invention. Finally, the proposed invention must be "useful." Legal experts commonly interpret this to mean that no patent will be granted for inventions that can only be used for an illegal or immoral purpose.

Some types of discoveries are not patentable. No one can obtain a patent on a law of nature or a scientific principle even if he or she is the first one to discover it. For example, Isaac Newton could not have obtained a patent on the laws of gravity, and Albert Einstein could not have patented his formula for relativity, $E=mc^2$.

—Adapted from Microsoft Encarta entry for "patent"

44. According to the passage, which of the following inventions would be considered most seriously for a patent by the U.S. Patent and Trademark Office (PTO)?

   (1) a new, successfully field-tested drug that is effective in treating asthma in young children
   (2) Faraday's discovery of electromagnetic induction, which made possible the electric generator
   (3) a recently revised and improved version of the Microsoft™ software for accountants and publishers
   (4) a best-selling novel about a lawyer's attempts to prosecute drug dealers in Kansas
   (5) a gadget that gives unauthorized people the capacity to desensitize security systems in banks

45. Through its intellectual property laws, what is the U.S. government placing value on?

   (1) competition
   (2) creativity
   (3) patriotism
   (4) intelligence
   (5) extravagance

Questions 46 and 47 refer to the brief passage and cartoon below.

On May 10, 1869, the Union Pacific and Central Pacific railroads met in Promontory, Utah to form the first transcontinental railway. The project had taken many years of hard labor to complete.

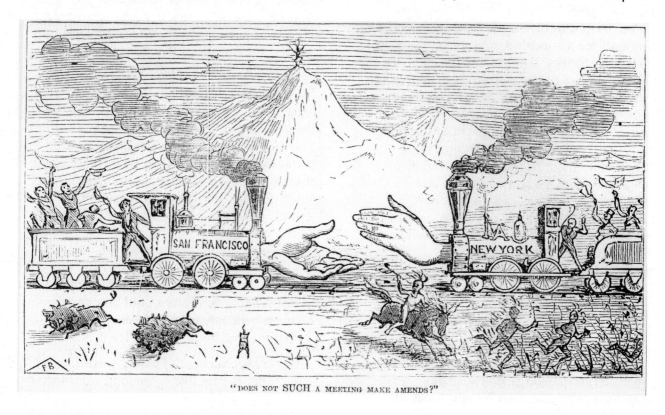

"DOES NOT SUCH A MEETING MAKE AMENDS?"

46. The caption of the cartoon reads, "Does not SUCH a meeting make amends?" From this question what can one infer about the building of the railroad?

(1) that there had been a constant feeling of goodwill and cooperation between the two railroad companies
(2) that the railroad companies had succeeded in their venture despite protests from environmentalists
(3) that few government officials supported the building of the railroad and contributed no federal funds
(4) that while there was reason to celebrate the railroad's completion, it had not been easily accomplished
(5) that people from New York would now be less likely to criticize those who had moved to San Francisco

47. Which of the following would *not* have been a result of the completion of the transcontinental railroad?

(1) Many laborers were injured or died while struggling to lay tracks over dangerous terrain.
(2) It became much easier for the West to obtain supplies and resources from the East.
(3) People who were interested in settling in the West now had a more efficient means of transportation.
(4) Native American tribes resented their lands' being granted to railroad companies.
(5) Train travel became too expensive for most Americans to afford and few people used the railway.

Question 48 refers to the bar graph below.

TOP INTERNET ROUTES

The data-carrying capability of the top international route of each region, measured in megabits per second

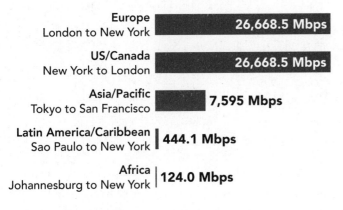

Europe
London to New York — 26,668.5 Mbps

US/Canada
New York to London — 26,668.5 Mbps

Asia/Pacific
Tokyo to San Francisco — 7,595 Mbps

Latin America/Caribbean
Sao Paulo to New York — 444.1 Mbps

Africa
Johannesburg to New York — 124.0 Mbps

48. Which of the following statements does the information in the bar graph support?

(1) The United States and Canada have more access to the Internet than any other region in the world.

(2) The graph illustrates reasons for the digital divide between highly developed countries and those still developing.

(3) The small Internet capability of Latin America and the Caribbean accounts for the poverty in much of that region.

(4) The statistic on Asia and the Pacific must not be correct since we know how technologically advanced Japan is.

(5) Most of the top Internet routes connect with Europe, meaning that Europe is the heart of the Internet.

Questions 49 and 50 are based on the following passage.

We are accustomed to think of the Renaissance as a period of cultural revival which fostered technological inventiveness and change. Certainly, clearer, more rational attitudes did create a background more favorable to systematic investigations. But the classical values which molded the Italian Renaissance were not favorable to applied technology. On the contrary, they emphasized the old distinction between science and technology: philosophical speculation was considered an attribute of gentility, while concern with practical matters was seen as a mark of vulgarity. Physicians strove to rank themselves as philosophers and to dissociate themselves from the surgeons, who were looked upon a technicians and therefore as low-class artisans. Architects worked tirelessly to dissociate themselves from engineers. However, the development of an urban, mercantile economy ultimately favored a utilitarian view of science and fostered a rapprochement between science and technology.

—Excerpted from *The Technology of Man* by Carlo M. Cipolla and Derek Birdsall

49. The distinction that the Renaissance made between the people engaged in science and those in technology was a reflection of which of the following social attitudes?

(1) racism
(2) sexism
(3) classism
(4) xenophobia
(5) homophobia

50. Which conclusion can one draw from the passage about the early years of the Renaissance?

(1) Philosophers were not highly respected.
(2) The economy was rural and agricultural.
(3) No technological advances were made.
(4) Architecture was considered a vulgar profession.
(5) Most people worked in large cities.

Answers are on pages 144–147.

Chapter 6
Global Connections

GED Social Studies pages 283–326
Complete GED pages 297–326

Questions 1 and 2 are based on the following passage.

On October 19, 1781, the British surrendered to the Americans at the Battle of Yorktown after six-and-a-half years of long winters, hand-to-hand battles, and the loss of many lives. The Revolutionary War is an example of a victory won by the side with fewer resources and soldiers, scarcer amounts of food, and less money. The American Army defeated the greatest superpower at that time by an abundance of spirit for the cause, strong leadership, and generous contributions of help and support from the French. Ultimately, too, Britain's lack of belief in its own cause contributed to its own defeat.

1. The colonists' position in the Revolutionary War was most similar to which of the following?

   (1) the resource-rich Americans fighting fascism during World War II
   (2) the powerful Russians trying to impose Communism in Afghanistan
   (3) the American-supported South Koreans during the Korean conflict
   (4) the impoverished but idealistic Vietcong during the Vietnam War
   (5) the government-controlled Chinese army during the Cultural Revolution

2. According to the passage, which country had the most powerful military in 1781?

   (1) the United States
   (2) France
   (3) Russia
   (4) Great Britain
   (5) Canada

Questions 3–6 are based on the following passage.

Approximately 170 countries exist today, and about 160 of them have constitutions based directly or indirectly on the United States model. Japan's, drafted with much American influence right after World War II, contains the unusual stipulation that Japan will never again wage war against other countries or even maintain an army, navy, or air force. Not all national charters have been as heavily dominated by the ideas or desires of the United States, however. In fact, most countries constantly rewrite their constitutions or ignore major principles in them in order to fit the political inclination of the current ruler.

3. Why do the Japanese spend only about 1% of their Gross National Product on defense?

   Because they
   (1) are dominated by American influence
   (2) have never engaged in a war
   (3) owe so much money to other countries
   (4) still have expenses from past wars
   (5) do not pay for armed services

4. Because of the fears of the return of dictatorships in Germany and Italy after World War II, the framers of their constitutions severely limited which of the following?

   (1) the power of the executive branch
   (2) the number of representatives in Parliament
   (3) the independence of the court system
   (4) the restrictions on the amendment process
   (5) the civil rights of individuals

87

5. With which of the following opinions would the writer of the passage most likely agree?

   (1) The United States should follow the example set by other countries that have changed constitutions about every 20 years.
   (2) The use of the United States Constitution as a model has led to problems of misinterpretation of its principles in other countries.
   (3) The United States Constitution is a unique document that has had a wide-ranging influence on politics around the world.
   (4) Japan's constitution should be used as the model for other countries because of its rule against waging war.
   (5) Americans were too harsh in their demand that Japan give up its support of an army, navy, and air force.

6. China's current constitution grants freedom of speech, the press, assembly, association, procession, and demonstration. Which of the following actions by the Beijing government directly contradicted one of the freedoms listed?

   (1) loosening the regulations about who could enter the country
   (2) shutting down production of several periodicals
   (3) allowing some movies to be made there by Westerners
   (4) not allowing the Dalai Lama to live in Tibet
   (5) maintaining strict control over the limited court system

Questions 7 and 8 are based on the following passage.

How would you like it if the United States government suddenly declared itself bankrupt? No longer would it make good on all those Treasury bills and Treasury bonds you, your neighbors, your parents, your banks, your insurance company, your pension fund, your school system, and employer have bought.

You want to start a depression real fast? Cause a worldwide crash? This would do it. No more jobs for anybody.

A default by the most powerful economy on the face of the earth would wipe out fortunes and destroy income instantly. The dollar would drop so low that even the Democratic Republic of Congo wouldn't buy it.

Churches wouldn't even accept it in the collection plate.

7. Which of the following is "the most powerful economy on the face of the Earth" referred to in the passage?

   (1) the Democratic Republic of the Congo
   (2) the United States of America
   (3) the Roman Catholic Church
   (4) the Treasury Department
   (5) the International Monetary Fund

8. From the facts presented in the passage, what can you infer about the Democratic Republic of Congo?

   It is
   (1) the poorest nation on the face of the Earth
   (2) the wealthiest and most powerful nation in Africa
   (3) a Third World nation plagued by poverty and underdevelopment
   (4) the one nation on Earth where the dollar's value is most respected
   (5) a poorly run nation that is always seeking handouts

Question 9 is based on the following passage.

According to the Electronics Industries Association, the United States loses more than $9 billion in business and 225,000 jobs every year because of export laws that forbid certain manufacturers to sell militarily sensitive electronic products to foreign countries.

9. Which of the following would benefit most from restrictions on the electronics exports described above?

(1) all foreign concerns that desire to buy American electronic products
(2) Japanese exporters who desire a greater share of the American electronics market
(3) the Commerce Department, which seeks to increase the flow of foreign-made electronics products
(4) the U.S. auto industry, which has problems similar to the Electronics Industries Association
(5) the Pentagon, which wants to have the world's most advanced electronic equipment

Questions 10–12 are based on the following graph.

10. The U.S. balance of trade with a country is the value of its exports to the country minus the value of its imports from that country. During the period shown on the graph, with which group(s) did the United States have the most consistent balance of trade?

(1) Canada
(2) Western Europe
(3) Japan
(4) Japan and Western Europe
(5) Western Europe and Canada

11. Over the years shown, which of the following best describes the U.S. balance of trade with Japan?

(1) It rose slightly.
(2) It declined steadily.
(3) It fluctuated but remained even overall.
(4) It fluctuated but declined overall.
(5) It fluctuated but eventually rose.

12. Which of the following might logically account for the decline in the general U.S. trade balance between 1991 and 1992?

The United States
(1) exported more goods abroad
(2) sold fewer goods abroad
(3) depended less on imported goods
(4) responded to a healthy stock market
(5) placed new restrictions on imports

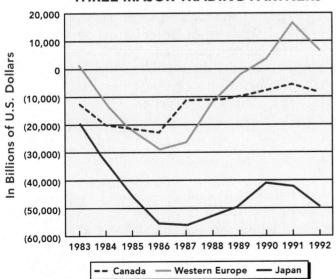

U.S. BALANCE OF TRADE WITH THREE MAJOR TRADING PARTNERS

Questions 13 and 14 are based on the following map.

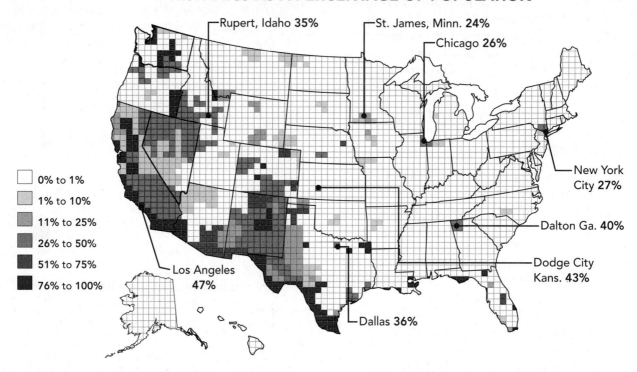

HISPANICS AS A PERCENTAGE OF POPULATION

Rupert, Idaho **35%**

St. James, Minn. **24%**

Chicago **26%**

New York City **27%**

Dalton Ga. **40%**

Dodge City Kans. **43%**

Los Angeles **47%**

Dallas **36%**

0% to 1%
1% to 10%
11% to 25%
26% to 50%
51% to 75%
76% to 100%

13. According to the map, where is the greatest concentration of Hispanics in the United States?

   (1) in major urban areas across the nation
   (2) along the United States-Mexico border
   (3) in southern and central California
   (4) along the east coast of the United States
   (5) in rural areas in the South and West

14. El Paso is a large city in western Texas on the Mexican border. The information on this map could be best used to support which policy in El Paso?

   (1) require that all government documents be only in English
   (2) restrict the amount of Mexican history and culture taught in schools
   (3) expand funding for English for Speakers of Other Languages classes
   (4) discontinue funding for Spanish classes in the public schools
   (5) establish a one-year moratorium on all new construction

Question 15 is based on the following letter to the editor.

The proposed missile-defense shield is irrelevant to the security of the U.S. and its allies [Nation, May 14]. Even if it were to work, a smart terrorist could surely find many cheap and easy ways to bypass it. Simply put, the "space shield" is the U.S.'s version of France's World War II Maginot Line, and it can be easily circumvented. Why wouldn't an enemy state just use an individual to smuggle a nuclear, chemical or biological device across our porous borders? U.S. security would be better served if the billions of dollars wasted on this illogical idea were used to bolster our National Guard and Reserve units.

—Excerpted from "Big-Ticket Boondoggle?,"
Time Magazine, June 4, 2001

15. Given the tone and information of this letter, what is probably the correct description of the French Maginot Line?

(1) It was an unsuccessful underground supply line for partisans fighting the Nazis.
(2) It was a secret production technique for producing weapons for the French army.
(3) It was a policy of conciliation and appeasement that the Nazis mistook for weakness.
(4) It was an early attempt to create a "space shield" to protect against foreign attack.
(5) It was a series of forts on the French-German border that the Nazis went around.

Question 16 is based on the following photograph.

16. Mahatma Gandhi was the leader of the independence movement in India. From this photo of him, what did he likely value most?

(1) impressing others
(2) holding political power
(3) controlling the lives of people
(4) producing his own clothes
(5) living simply and humbly

Questions 17 and 18 are based on the following passage and chart.

[More than] ten years ago the Exxon Valdez ran aground on a reef and spilled 11 million gallons of crude oil into Alaska's Prince William Sound. It was a devastating tragedy and it got a lot of press, but far more oil enters the environment from less dramatic incidents. Just because a spill is not concentrated doesn't mean it's harmless; the amount of oil from an average oil change could kill fish in a million gallons of water. Here is how much oil is released into the environment each year, worldwide, as reported by the National Research Council and measured in Exxon Valdez increments:

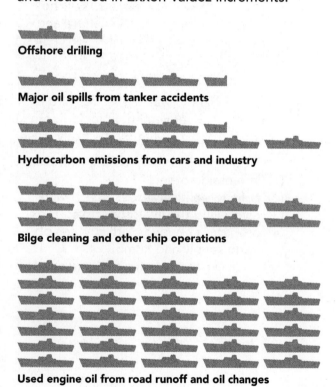

Offshore drilling

Major oil spills from tanker accidents

Hydrocarbon emissions from cars and industry

Bilge cleaning and other ship operations

Used engine oil from road runoff and oil changes

= 11 million gallons of oil, the amount spilled by the Exxon Valdez

—Excerpted from "We All Live on the Exxon Valdez," *Sierra*, March/April 1999

17. According to the information in the passage and chart, what is the greatest threat to the environment?

   (1) offshore drilling
   (2) major oil spills from tanker accidents
   (3) hydrocarbon emissions from cars and industry
   (4) bilge cleaning and other ship operations
   (5) used engine oil from road runoff and oil changes

18. Which change would be most likely to have the greatest effect in reducing the amount of oil released into the environment?

   (1) recycling used oil from vehicle oil changes
   (2) only allowing double-hulled tankers
   (3) imposing stricter limits on hydrocarbon emissions
   (4) increasing offshore oil exploration and drilling
   (5) requiring ships to do bilge cleaning while at sea

Questions 19 and 20 are based on the following passage.

If you want to understand the gold rush, you've got to know the prospectors. The reason that Laredo and nearby McAllen, Texas, are two of the top 10 fastest-growing metro areas in the U.S. is mainly owing to NAFTA and its progeny: NAFTA Man.

NAFTA Man is not only bilingual, he's also bicultural. He speaks Spanish on the factory floor in Mexico but yells in English at his kids' T-ball games. He knows when to offer a bribe in Mexico (to a traffic cop) and when not to (during an environmental inspection). He prefers chile rellenos to pot roast, gets his allergy medicine in Mexico but his MRI in the U.S. He has a two-sided wallet for pesos and dollars and would practically kill for a cell phone that works in both countries. "We don't know who we are," laughs John Castany, president of the Reynosa Maquiladora Association, which has 110 mostly gringo members. "We're schizo. Border culture is just, well, different."

These NAFTA Men—and a few women— are genetically engineered by the new border economy. Managers are taught to take a different route to work every day to foil potential kidnappers. They grow accustomed to training—and losing—an entire factory floor of workers every year. And they have discovered that "casual Friday" in McAllen is often a dress-up workday on the other side. Around here, the most valuable asset is their flexibility. "You have to switch gears in Mexico—and not just languages. You have a behavior shift too," says Charles Taliaferro, 49, who runs maquila operations for Am-Mex Products, which makes everything from Siemens electric motors to Smead file folders. Workers cause less trouble, but their bosses have to be more considerate. "In Mexico, you're more polite, more formal," he says.

—Excerpted from "The Rise of the NAFTA Manager," *Time Magazine*, June 11, 2001

19. Which of the following policies would NAFTA Man be most likely to support?

(1) English-only legislation to ban the use of Spanish in the United States
(2) tighter restrictions on travel across the U.S.-Mexican border
(3) the repeal of NAFTA in order to protect American jobs
(4) increased funding for more border crossings into Mexico
(5) stricter penalties for smuggling illegal drugs into the United States

20. NAFTA Man is most similar to which of the following?

(1) the Ugly American, who makes no effort to learn the local culture and language of the country in which he is working
(2) the child of an immigrant to the United States who tries to adopt American culture and forget his own culture
(3) a businessman in India, who speaks English and is comfortable with Indian culture
(4) a resident of the Netherlands who works in Belgium and is comfortable with the languages and cultures of both countries
(5) a Canadian who lives in Windsor, Ontario and works in a factory in Detroit, Michigan

Questions 21 and 22 are based on the following passage.

"We have uncovered a strong link between conditions affecting agriculture and poverty and the new types of conflict," says Indra de Soysa, co-author along with Nils Peter Gleditsch, of the report titled *To Cultivate Peace: Agriculture in a World of Conflict.* "These new conflicts can be traced to the loss of livelihood, the hopelessness of surviving at the margins and the alternative life of crime and banditry."

"It is much less expensive to provide poor nations with technical agricultural assistance now rather than rushing in emergency food aid to war-ravaged regions later," says Dr. Ismail Serageldin, World Bank Vice President for Special Programs and chair of CGIAR.

The report shows that when people are unable to meet food requirements and other basic needs, their survival strategies become more desperate and many join rebellions or become criminals.

The report identifies three new patterns of warfare:

1. These new wars are largely internal, reflect crises of subsistence and are usually apolitical. They derive from the failure of development, the loss of livelihood and the collapse of states. These new conflicts do not follow the model of the Cold War era of 1945–89 when ideological considerations and superpower rivalry sparked most hostilities around the world.

2. Because the wars are being fought over poverty and food security issues, the victims are civilians rather than supporters of armed movements.

3. These wars have been extraordinarily violent, often because of the land issues or the ethnic rivalry involved, with much of the brutality committed on the most vulnerable of noncombatants—women, children and the elderly. Part of the violence is the technique of willful

famine, which has been used to kill en masse in such countries as Liberia, Mozambique, Somalia and the Sudan.

—Excerpted from *Calypso* Log, April 1999

21. According to the information in this passage, which aid program would probably have the greatest long-term benefit to a poor country?

    (1) an emergency food aid program run by CARE for displaced refugees
    (2) a seed-distribution and farmer-training program run by the Carter Center
    (3) a letter writing campaign by Amnesty International protesting atrocities
    (4) a foreign aid program by the United States to fund a new steel mill
    (5) an artificial-limb program for war victims run by Doctors Without Borders

22. All except which of the following conflicts follow the model of new patterns of warfare described in this passage?

    (1) the civil war in the Ivory Coast in which rebels routinely mutilate and cut off the limbs of civilians
    (2) the invasion of Kosovo by the Yugoslav army during which thousands of ethnic Albanians were killed
    (3) the war in the Congo in which more than 2 million have died while valuable resources have been plundered
    (4) the Gulf War in which a coalition of forces led by the U.S. drove Saddam Hussein's army out of Kuwait
    (5) the Bosnian War in which both Serbs and Croats engaged in ethnic cleansing against Muslims and each other

Question 23 is based on the following photograph and caption.

Demonstrators hurl rocks at Soviet tanks when they move in to put down an anti-Communist uprising in East Berlin.

23. What was the most likely reason the demonstrators were throwing rocks at the Soviet tanks?

(1) They were trying to damage the tanks so that they could not operate.

(2) They were trying to divert the tanks from important targets.

(3) They were expressing rage and frustration at the Soviet invasion.

(4) They wanted the Soviets to clean up the mess they were making.

(5) They were trying to stir up trouble and disrupt the peace.

Questions 24 and 25 are based on the following photograph.

24. What aspect of this photograph makes it most shocking?

(1) the use of the American flag as a weapon

(2) the depiction of unprovoked violence

(3) its example of racial intolerance

(4) the fact that it is happening in a public place

(5) the onlookers' failure to assist the victim

25. What most likely was the point of view of the photographer?

(1) supportive of the attacker who was opposed to school busing

(2) eager to promote a positive image for the city of Boston

(3) understanding of the importance of documenting this expression of hatred

(4) understanding of the importance of racial separation in order to keep peace

(5) supportive of the integration of all Boston Public Schools

Question 26 is based on the following photograph.

Question 27 is based on the following photograph.

27. While this image was taken at an Albanian refugee camp during the war in Kosovo, what is its universal message?

(1) War creates enormous suffering and deprivation.
(2) Children should not be kept in camps during a war.
(3) Conflict can help build resourcefulness and character.
(4) The United Nations should ban the use of fences.
(5) Children should be evacuated from areas of conflict.

26. This photograph is of public buildings in Brasilia, the capital of Brazil. From the design of these structures, what can you infer was probably the most important value to the planners and builders of this city?

(1) keeping a human scale
(2) projecting warmth and caring
(3) promoting modernity and progress
(4) relating to Brazil's rich heritage
(5) serving those most in need

Go to **www.GEDSocialStudies.com** for additional practice and instruction!

Questions 28–30 are based on the following passage.

Before reading *King Leopold's Ghost*, I was unaware of the holocaust that occurred in Central Africa between 1880 and 1920. I didn't know that Leopold, King of the Belgians, had carved out the vast territory around the Congo River as his own personal colony, imposing a forced-labor system to exploit the region's natural resources. And I had no idea that a popular movement had risen up in revulsion at the horrors of the Congo, launching the first international human rights campaign of the modern era.

According to estimates cited by Hochschild, fully half of the Congolese population perished during Leopold's rule and its aftermath. In other words, 8 million to 10 million human lives were taken directly or indirectly by the king's agents and mercenaries, including the private army he employed, the Force Publique.

Amazingly, Leopold himself never set foot in the Congo. Instead, he orchestrated the colony's systematic rape from the comfort of royal estates in Brussels and elsewhere. In the service of his vast fortune (an estimated $1.1 billion in today's dollars), many of the Congo's indigenous people were worked to death as porters and gatherers of ivory and wild rubber. Others died of starvation and exposure after soldiers burned their villages and stole their livestock.

—Excerpted from "The Politics of Forgetting" by Tim Ledwith, *Amnesty Action*, Spring 1999

28. Leopold's troops were ordered to cut off the right hand of each person they had killed in order to show that they had not "wasted" a bullet. From this information, what can you conclude the troops valued most?

(1) saving the lives of the Congolese people in any way possible
(2) accounting for their bullets even if it meant mutilating people
(3) the obedience and cooperation of the Congolese people
(4) the productivity of the indigenous Congolese population
(5) the health and welfare of the local Congolese laborers

29. In 1880, what was the approximate population of the Congo?

(1) 8 million
(2) 9 million
(3) 10 million
(4) 18 million
(5) 36 million

30. School textbooks in Belgium used to claim that Leopold was a benign ruler whose stewardship of the Congo was guided by "humanitarian" concerns. This fact, along with the information in the passage, leads to which of the following conclusions?

(1) The writer was unaware of what had happened in the Congo.
(2) An international human rights campaign protested Leopold's abuses.
(3) The Belgians tried to cover up the extent of their abuses in the Congo.
(4) Many native Congolese were worked to death or died of starvation.
(5) Leopold's forces treated the indigenous Congolese very brutally.

Question 31 is based on the following photograph and caption.

Jerry Rawlings, president of Ghana, appears with U.S. President Bill Clinton and First Lady Hillary Rodham Clinton before a huge crowd in Independence Square in Accra, Ghana's capital, on March 23, 1998. The Clintons are wearing traditional Asante textiles called kente cloth.

31. Which is the most likely explanation for why the Clintons were wearing kente cloth in this photo?

(1) They were showing that they were good sports who could take a joke.
(2) They thought that the cloth was very beautiful and wanted to publicly promote it.
(3) They thought they would look fashionable combining African and western clothing.
(4) They were impressed by the quality of workmanship and creative design in the fabric.
(5) They wanted to show solidarity with the people of Ghana and respect for their culture.

Questions 32 and 33 are based on the following cartoon.

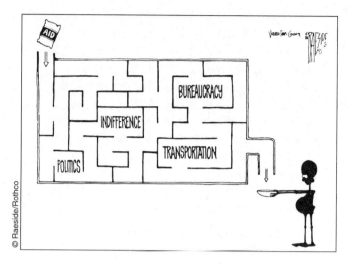

© Raeside/Rothco

32. What is the main point of this cartoon?

(1) Aid must travel through a difficult maze to get to the recipient.
(2) It's important to support international relief organizations.
(3) Not enough aid is being donated to help the hungry.
(4) Safeguards are needed to ensure that aid is not wasted.
(5) Food aid is not as important as helping people help themselves.

33. Of the following proposals, which would most directly address the issue being raised by this cartoon?

(1) organizing a major fundraising campaign to increase aid donations
(2) increasing government regulation and oversight of all relief efforts
(3) converting wild land into additional crop land for agriculture
(4) cutting red tape for organizations that can provide and deliver aid
(5) requiring all relief workers to provide extensive reports of their activities

Questions 34 and 35 are based on the following photograph and passage.

It's the dome that does it. This architectural wedding cake celebrating the union of the states may be the best mood elevator available without a prescription. I don't know how it works or why. All I know is that looking at it takes me out of myself to a better place.

Abraham Lincoln understood that well. The dome was half finished when the Civil War erupted. There were some who thought that construction funds would be better spent on bullets and bayonets, but Lincoln wanted the dome completed as a symbol of the permanence of the Union and, by implication, of confidence in better days to come. The president prevailed, the work went on. Today, enshrined at the other end of the Mall, Lincoln must take enormous satisfaction in the symbol that he insisted be realized.

34. All except which of the following structures have an impact similar to that described in the passage?

(1) the Eiffel Tower in Paris, France
(2) the Empire State Building in New York City
(3) the Taj Mahal in Agra, India
(4) the childhood home of Abraham Lincoln
(5) the Golden Gate Bridge in California

35. According to the information in this passage, what did Abraham Lincoln think was the most important?

(1) spending all available resources on weapons and ammunition
(2) creating a monument of the Union to build morale
(3) enlisting the assistance of black slaves in the war effort
(4) having a memorial built for himself in sight of the Capitol
(5) having the half-built dome stand for a nation torn in two

Questions 36 and 37 are based on the following passage.

The Carpet Slaves follows Chichai, a subsistence farmer in northern India, as he searches for his 11-year-old son, Huro, who disappeared in 1994. Chichai believes that the boy was kidnapped by a rugmaker and forced to work as many as 20 hours a day without wages. He travels to India's rug belt and, after a daring raid on a notorious shop, finds his son, who is malnourished and frightened and no longer speaks the same language as his family. The film's best—and most agonizing—moment comes when Chichai admits that though Huro is home, he still seems lost.

The filmmakers make clear that Huro and Chichai's story is not merely a local tragedy and that child servitude is the dark side of globalization. The rugs that child slaves make are sold in stores around the world, and the boys' work feeds a global appetite for cheap goods. Woods and Blewett's message is fairly simple: Don't buy anything without knowing its origin. Like Huro's transition to freedom, that may be easier said than done.

—This excerpt is from an article that first appeared in the April, 2001 edition of *Brill's Content* magazine. It is reprinted with permission.

36. According to the information in this article, what is the most important consideration of consumers when they buy something?

(1) the quality of the workmanship
(2) getting a bargain price
(3) concern for the workers
(4) promoting social change
(5) maintaining the status quo

37. The filmmakers Woods and Blewett would be most likely to support which of the following?

(1) a free service that would search for and find the lowest price for a product
(2) relaxing child-labor laws in the United States so that young people can get job experience
(3) boycotting companies that market products manufactured through child slave labor
(4) a television program in which the owners of the rug-making shop tells his side of the story
(5) a marketing campaign that would promote products manufactured in India

Questions 38 and 39 are based on the following map.

GREEK COLONIZATION c. 750-500 B.C.

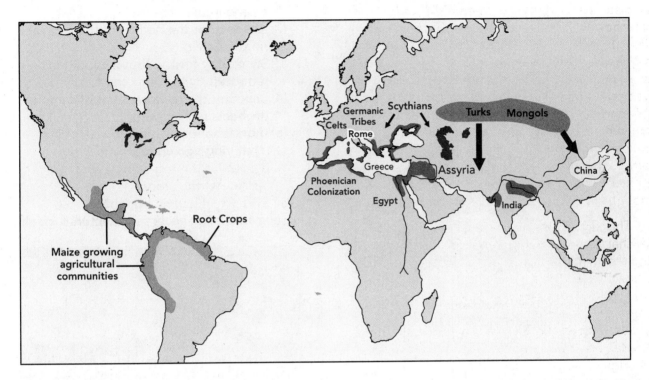

38. According to the information in this map, which of the following events was happening at the same time that the ancient Greeks were colonizing the Mediterranean Sea and Black Sea?

(1) China was threatening other parts of the world with invasion.
(2) Advanced civilizations were flourishing in the Americas.
(3) Northern Europe was one of the most advanced parts of the world.
(4) Agrarian societies were developing in Central and South America.
(5) North America was more developed than South America.

39. Looking at the areas of the earth that were most developed by 500 B.C.E., which hypothesis is best supported by the map?

(1) People of Caucasian ancestry were most likely to be the most developed.
(2) Many early civilizations developed as a way of dealing with cold climates.
(3) Most ancient civilizations grew near bodies of water such as seas or rivers.
(4) The modern distribution of power in the world was already evident in 500 B.C.E.
(5) International trade had led to the growth of civilization around the world.

Questions 40 and 41 are based on the following photograph and caption.

Two caravans on 30-day treks pass in the desert in Niger, one heading toward Bilma to load up on salt, a precious commodity, the other returning to markets at the edge of the Sahara.

40. This photograph was taken at the end of the twentieth century. Which of the following is a fact that can be determined from this information, the photograph, and the caption?

(1) Camels will always remain the main means of transportation in the Sahara.
(2) Salt is too valuable to be transported by trucks or other motorized vehicles.
(3) Camel caravans like this will soon become extinct and be replaced by trains.
(4) Working in a camel caravan is a very desirable job in the Sahara.
(5) Modern development has not yet come to this portion of the Sahara.

41. What was most likely the point of view of the photographer of this photograph?

(1) contempt for the primitiveness of the scene in the desert
(2) respect for the beauty of the caravans in the desert
(3) sympathy for the brutal conditions endured by the workers
(4) alarm at the mistreatment of camels as beasts of burden
(5) nostalgia for a time and way of life that long ago ended

Question 42 is based on the following photograph.

IT IS BETTER TO HAVE ONE CHILD ONLY

42. What is the most likely purpose of this billboard in China?

(1) to improve the productivity of workers
(2) to reduce the rate of population increase
(3) to encourage families to keep their daughters
(4) to support the nuclear family
(5) to improve the country's child-care system

Questions 43 and 44 are based on the following graph and political cartoon.

WORLD POPULATION GROWTH
1750–2100

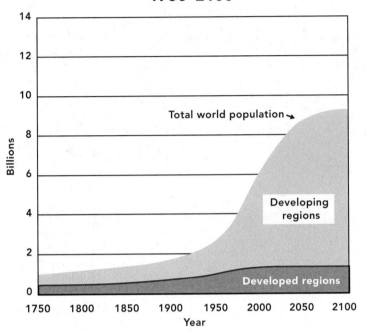

Source: *Population Reference Bureau estimates, 1990.*

43. What conclusion could be drawn from either the cartoon or the graph?

(1) Almost all population growth in the next century will be in developing countries.
(2) Population growth leveled off in developed regions by the end of the twentieth century.
(3) Poor, developing countries are dealing with a huge increase in population.
(4) Overpopulation is preventing poor countries from reaching food sufficiency.
(5) World population is expected to level off by the end of the twenty-first century.

44. According to the artist of the cartoon, what is the single most important barrier to economic progress in poor countries?

(1) an overabundance of water
(2) too many people to feed
(3) incurable fatal diseases
(4) a lack of determination
(5) insufficient foreign investment

'We can't seem to keep our heads above water'...

Questions 45 and 46 are based on the following map.

EXPANSION OF ISLAM c. 632–1000 A.D.

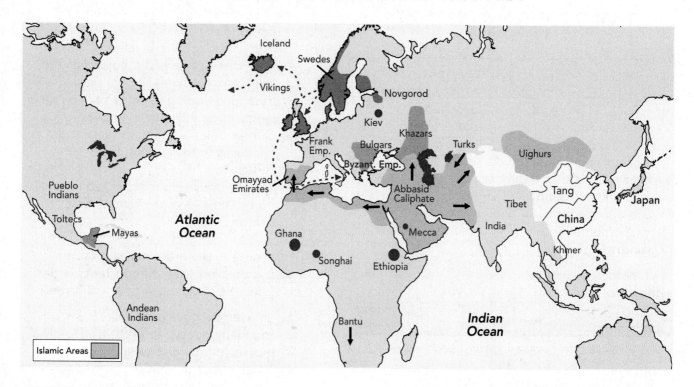

45. Which of the following countries was Islamic during the time period shown on this map, but is not an Islamic country today?

   (1) Russia
   (2) Iran
   (3) Spain
   (4) Morocco
   (5) Tibet

46. During the period depicted in the map, all but which of the following were occurring?

   (1) The Mayan Civilization was developing in Central America.
   (2) Islam was expanding across India and North Africa, and into Europe.
   (3) The Bantu were expanding south in Sub-Saharan Africa.
   (4) Christianity was spreading across the North Atlantic to North America.
   (5) Tang China was one of the world's great empires.

Questions 47 and 48 are based on the following passage.

Gasoline is refined from crude oil, which remains Asia's main source of energy. Since the region does not produce enough oil for its own purposes, it has to import most of it.

While expensive crude oil imports remain the prime reason for the push, the search for alternatives has recently been kicked into overdrive because toxic emissions from vehicles were found to be the leading cause of air pollution in Asia. Vehicle emissions pose a greater threat than industrial emissions as they are close to ground level and are constantly swirled in the air by passing traffic, said senior environmental engineer with the World Bank, Jitendra Shah.

"Much needs to be done if you look at the air quality trend in cities such as Manila, Jakarta and Dhaka. It's not getting any better," Shah said.

According to the World Health Organization, four to eight percent of all deaths in the Asia-Pacific region are due to air pollution.

This prompted the World Bank and the Asian Development Bank to launch a Clean Air Initiative in February with officials from eight Asian countries.

The programme strives to share knowledge and expedite pilot air-quality projects through a series of workshops.

So from Pakistan to China, Asian governments are trying to encourage the use of different types of alternative fuels.

Pakistan and Australia have turned to natural gas, either in compressed or liquefied form, because of its relative abundance in those countries while resource-poor countries such as Singapore are pursuing fuel-cell technology.

A fuel cell is an electrochemical device that combines hydrogen fuel and oxygen from the air to produce electricity, which can power a car.

Other countries such as China, India and Thailand are looking at biofuels.

The two most common biofuels are ethanol and biodiesel, a diesel-engine fuel that can be made from vegetable oils, animal fat or algae.

Thailand has even explored the use of coconut oil and palm oil, with King Bhumibol Adulyadej taking an interest in the latter by patenting a palm oil formula at the beginning of May.

The formula, which consists of one part crude palm oil and nine parts diesel, can easily power vehicles with no harm to the engine, said the state-run Petroleum Authority of Thailand, which conducts tests for the king.

47. According to the information in this passage, which scenario is most likely to occur in Asia?

    (1) There will be a major push to find new oil fields for exploitation.
    (2) Coconut oil and palm oil will replace crude oil as the main source of energy.
    (3) Alternatives to crude oil will be developed and marketed.
    (4) Pollution in Asia will be successfully controlled.
    (5) Asia will become the world's leading producer of alternative energy.

48. What is the main idea of this passage?

    (1) Asian nations are exploring alternative energy sources to reduce energy imports and pollution.
    (2) The king of Thailand is an inventor who has patented a formula combining palm oil and diesel.
    (3) Asia must import crude oil in order to meet its growing energy needs.
    (4) Pollution from burning gasoline has had a severe negative impact on public health in Asia.
    (5) The development of alternative fuels will eventually decrease the need for crude oil as an energy source.

Questions 49 and 50 refer to the cartoon below.

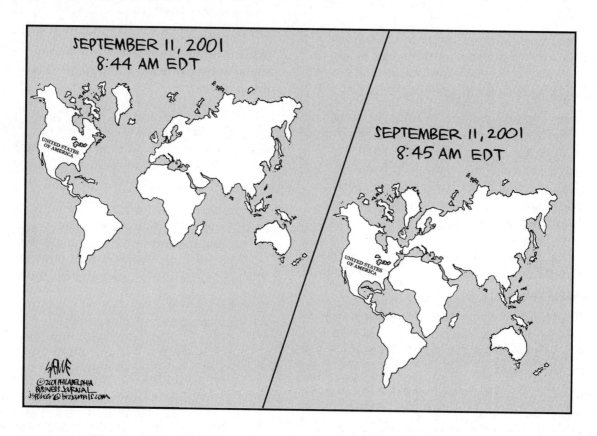

49. On September 11, 2001 at 8:45 AM, terrorists flew a commercial airliner into the North Tower of the World Trade Center in New York City, beginning the worst attack in the continental United States since the Civil War over 100 hundred years ago. What was the cartoonist trying to convey with the two maps about this event?

(1) The continents can move much faster than we realize.
(2) The United States is much closer to Africa than previously thought.
(3) The United States is no more protected than the rest of the world.
(4) The United States has weapons that can reach anywhere in the world.
(5) Nobody can ever be safe from the threat of fanatical terrorists.

50. By drawing this cartoon to depict the horrible events of September 11, 2001, what was the concept the cartoonist was trying to illustrate?

(1) the terror felt by the victims of the attacks in the USA
(2) the empathy people everywhere felt for Americans
(3) the need of many Americans for vengeance
(4) the importance of patrolling all our borders
(5) the enormity of the crimes of the terrorists

Answers are on pages 147–150.

Social Studies

Directions: This model test will help you identify the skills you will need in order to be successful on the new 2002 GED Social Studies Test. This test consists of fifty multiple-choice questions and should take no longer than 70 minutes to complete. The questions are based on passages, graphs, charts, maps, political cartoons, and photographs pertaining to all areas of social studies: U.S. history, world history, geography, economics, and civics and government.

When you complete the test, check your work using the answers and explanations at the end of the test. Use the evaluation chart on page 131 to determine the areas in which you will need more study before taking the 2002 GED Social Studies Test.

Model Test Answer Grid

1	① ② ③ ④ ⑤		18	① ② ③ ④ ⑤		35	① ② ③ ④ ⑤
2	① ② ③ ④ ⑤		19	① ② ③ ④ ⑤		36	① ② ③ ④ ⑤
3	① ② ③ ④ ⑤		20	① ② ③ ④ ⑤		37	① ② ③ ④ ⑤
4	① ② ③ ④ ⑤		21	① ② ③ ④ ⑤		38	① ② ③ ④ ⑤
5	① ② ③ ④ ⑤		22	① ② ③ ④ ⑤		39	① ② ③ ④ ⑤
6	① ② ③ ④ ⑤		23	① ② ③ ④ ⑤		40	① ② ③ ④ ⑤
7	① ② ③ ④ ⑤		24	① ② ③ ④ ⑤		41	① ② ③ ④ ⑤
8	① ② ③ ④ ⑤		25	① ② ③ ④ ⑤		42	① ② ③ ④ ⑤
9	① ② ③ ④ ⑤		26	① ② ③ ④ ⑤		43	① ② ③ ④ ⑤
10	① ② ③ ④ ⑤		27	① ② ③ ④ ⑤		44	① ② ③ ④ ⑤
11	① ② ③ ④ ⑤		28	① ② ③ ④ ⑤		45	① ② ③ ④ ⑤
12	① ② ③ ④ ⑤		29	① ② ③ ④ ⑤		46	① ② ③ ④ ⑤
13	① ② ③ ④ ⑤		30	① ② ③ ④ ⑤		47	① ② ③ ④ ⑤
14	① ② ③ ④ ⑤		31	① ② ③ ④ ⑤		48	① ② ③ ④ ⑤
15	① ② ③ ④ ⑤		32	① ② ③ ④ ⑤		49	① ② ③ ④ ⑤
16	① ② ③ ④ ⑤		33	① ② ③ ④ ⑤		50	① ② ③ ④ ⑤
17	① ② ③ ④ ⑤		34	① ② ③ ④ ⑤			

PRACTICE TEST

Questions 1–4 refer to the following section from the Declaration of Independence.

"The history of the present King of Great Britain is a history of repeated injuries and usurpations, all having in direct object the establishment of an absolute tyranny over these states. To prove this, let facts be submitted to a candid world.

"He has refused his assent to laws, the most wholesome and necessary for the public good. . . .

"He has dissolved representative houses repeatedly, for opposing, with manly firmness, his invasions on the rights of the people."

1. What is the purpose of this section of the Declaration of Independence?

   (1) to state that the colonies have formed an independent country
   (2) to explain why the new government does not have a king
   (3) to justify the colonies' decision to alter their form of government
   (4) to ask the king to show more respect for the rights of the colonists
   (5) to seek the help of France in waging war against Great Britain

2. Which of these phrases from the selection most clearly shows the author's persuasive intent?

   (1) in direct object
   (2) an absolute tyranny
   (3) a candid world
   (4) his assent to laws
   (5) representative houses

3. Years after this declaration was written, attitudes toward the King of Great Britain helped shape the Constitution that was written in 1787. Which of these Constitutional ideas was most likely a result of those attitudes?

   (1) a legislative body composed of two houses
   (2) political parties that organize legislative bodies
   (3) checks and balances
   (4) concurrent powers
   (5) direct election of the president

4. What purpose does the phrase *manly firmness* serve in this document?

   (1) It suggests that the colonists are strongly united in opposition to the king.
   (2) It illustrates that women were then excluded from the political process.
   (3) It proves that the king had broken his word.
   (4) It persuades the reader that the king had acted unlawfully.
   (5) It shows the colonists hoped for "a government of men, not angels."

PRACTICE TEST

Questions 5 and 6 refer to the following passage and map.

The Compromise of 1850

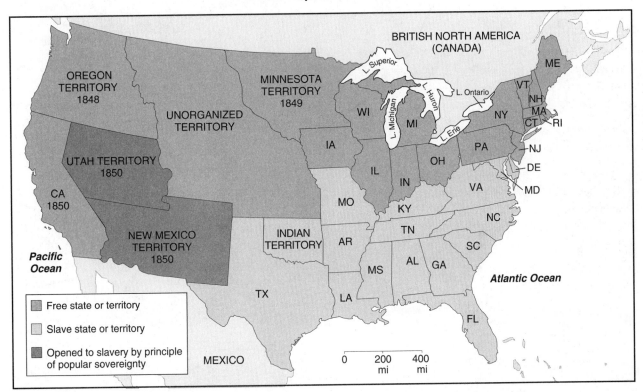

The Compromise of 1850 provided a temporary solution to the divisions between the North and the South. Proposed by Henry Clay, the aging Senator from Kentucky, the Compromise was an "omnibus" bill, designed to provide something to each side. California would be admitted as a free state, the territories of New Mexico and Utah would use popular sovereignty to decide on slave or free status, and the Texas-New Mexico boundary dispute would be settled.

In addition, the slave trade would be abolished in the District of Columbia, and a more effective Fugitive Slave Law would be passed. After much wrangling, Stephen A. Douglas of Illinois managed to get these provisions passed as separate bills in the summer of 1850.

5. Which provision of the Compromise of 1850 was primarily designed to appeal to Southerners?

   (1) the admission of California
   (2) the use of popular sovereignty in New Mexico and Utah
   (3) the settlement of the Texas boundary dispute
   (4) the abolition of the slave trade in the District of Columbia
   (5) the strengthening of the Fugitive Slave Law

6. Looking at the map, what can you see that created the need for the Compromise of 1850?

   (1) westward expansion of the United States
   (2) rise of the industrial cities of the North
   (3) existence of British control of Canada
   (4) extension of the railroad across the continent
   (5) imperialist moves of Spain in the Southwest

PRACTICE TEST

Questions 7–9 refer to the following cartoon.

In this British cartoon from 1898, Uncle Sam is dining on Cuba, "Porto" Rico, and the Philippine Islands. The other countries are dividing up China. England says, "We can't grudge him a light lunch while we are feasting."

7. Who does the figure seated at the right represent?

(1) Spain
(2) American industry
(3) the League of Nations
(4) the United States
(5) the British Empire

8. What can one assume about the period of history in which this cartoon was drawn?

(1) Cuba, Puerto Rico, and the Philippines were centers of the North American slave trade.
(2) China was weak, not the powerful, independent nation that it is today.
(3) Europe was not interested in Cuba because it was much further away than China.
(4) Most Europeans didn't know how to speak Spanish, but they did know Chinese.
(5) The United States was also keenly interested in having a piece of the Chinese pie.

PRACTICE TEST

9. What does the cartoonist seem to think about United States imperialism?

(1) It was a relatively small matter compared to European imperialism.
(2) It was greedily eating up territory all over the globe.
(3) It had few supporters among the American people.
(4) It had taken more than its fair share of the world's resources.
(5) It sacrificed the spirit of liberty on which the country was founded.

Question 10 refers to the following quote from George Washington's Farewell Address given to the nation in 1797.

"Promote, then, as an object of primary importance, institutions for the general diffusion of knowledge. In proportion as the structure of government gives force to public opinion, it is essential that public opinion should be enlightened."

10. Which of the following developments in American history best illustrate Washington's point?

(1) government censorship of the news during times of war
(2) the widening of the franchise so that more people could vote
(3) the establishment of public universities
(4) the expansion of the railroads in the West
(5) the widening of sectional differences before the Civil War

Question 11 refers to the following circle graphs.

Resources of the Union and Confederacy

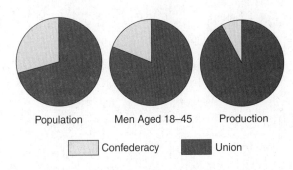

| Population | Men Aged 18–45 | Production |

□ Confederacy   ■ Union

11. What do these circle graphs show about the relative strengths of the Union and the Confederacy at the beginning of the Civil War?

(1) The Confederacy had more people but the Union had more material.
(2) The Confederacy had the dominant position in both men and material.
(3) The Union had the dominant position in both men and material.
(4) The Union had more people but the Confederacy had more material.
(5) The two sides were more or less evenly matched.

PRACTICE TEST

Questions 12 and 13 refer to the following bar graph.

**Popular Vote Cast for President, by
Major Political Party: 1980 to 1996**

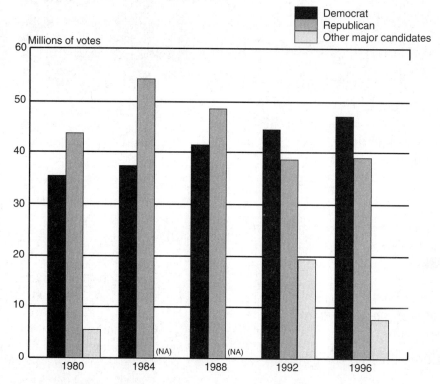

Source: U.S. Census Bureau

12. In several of these elections, third parties played a role. In which of these years was the result most affected by the third party vote?

(1) 1980
(2) 1984
(3) 1988
(4) 1992
(5) 1996

13. Which of the following statements can be inferred as true from the information in the graph?

(1) The participation of other parties alters the results of elections.
(2) There are more Republicans than Democrats in the United States.
(3) A large majority of Americans voted for the Republican candidate in 1984.
(4) The two major political parties did not change much between 1980 and 1996.
(5) Democratic candidates received a steady increase in votes between 1980 and 1996.

Questions 14 and 15 refer to the following passage.

The name "United Nations" was devised by U.S. President Franklin D. Roosevelt and was first used in the "Declaration by United Nations" January 1, 1942, during the Second World War, when representatives of 26 nations pledged to continue fighting together against the Axis powers.

The United Nations Charter was drawn up by the representatives of 50 countries at the United Nations Conference on International Organization, which met at San Francisco from April 25 to June 26, 1945. Those delegates deliberated at Dumbarton Oaks from August to October, 1944, on the basis of proposals worked out by the representatives of China, the Soviet Union, the United Kingdom, and the United States. The Charter was signed June 26, 1945, by the representatives of the 50 countries. Poland signed it later and became one of the original 51 member states.

The United Nations officially came into existence October 24, 1945, when the Charter had been ratified by China, France, the Soviet Union, the United Kingdom, the United States, and a majority of other countries. United Nations Day is celebrated on October 24 each year.

14. The process for creating the United Nations most closely resembled which of the following?

   (1) elections in a democratic country
   (2) the coronation of a monarch
   (3) the signing of the Declaration of Independence
   (4) the Constitutional Convention
   (5) the implementation of the Magna Carta

15. Germany is a powerful state in the world today, yet it was not included in the discussions at Dumbarton Oaks. Why was Germany not included?

   (1) Germany was not a powerful state at that time.
   (2) Great Britain was representing all the nations of Europe.
   (3) The nations at Dumbarton Oaks all had larger populations than Germany did.
   (4) The nations at Dumbarton Oaks were at war with Germany.
   (5) Germany had been invited, but did not participate because of political unrest at home.

PRACTICE TEST

Question 16 refers to the following photograph of the Berlin Wall.

On the afternoon of November 10, 1989, East and West Germans stood together on top of the Berlin Wall.

16. Which of the following would be the *least* appropriate title for this photograph?

    (1) Democracy Prevails!
    (2) Power to the People!
    (3) Here's to the Soviets!
    (4) Warmth after Cold!
    (5) Germany, United Once More!

PRACTICE TEST

Questions 17–19 refer to the following passage about Sparta.

Today the word *spartan* describes discipline, rigor, and discomfort. The ancient Greek city-state of Sparta, from which the term comes, had a way of life based on military strength that the Spartans needed to control the people they had enslaved.

Some of the people conquered by the Spartans were called *periokoi;* they had no citizenship rights, had to pay taxes, and served in the army. Unlike the conquered people called *helots,* the periokoi were not slaves. The helots, who outnumbered the Spartans, belonged to the community as a whole; they were forced to work in Spartan fields and homes. The historian Xenophon said the helots' feelings about the Spartans were, "They said they would be glad to eat them raw."

Spartan military strength depended on the strict training of Spartan youth, both male and female. Boys left home at the age of 7 for rigorous training called the *agoge.* Those who survived their childhood training became *homoioi,* entitled to respect and full participation in politics.

Spartan girls and women had far more freedom than other Greek females. Girls exercised with the boys, and women controlled their households. Since the housework was done by helots, Spartan women concentrated on raising healthy children with Spartan values.

17. What was the name given to a slave in Sparta?

   (1) periokoi
   (2) helot
   (3) Xenophon
   (4) agoge
   (5) homoioi

18. In which modern institution would you most likely find Spartan conditions?

   (1) a bank
   (2) an art school
   (3) an army barracks
   (4) a political campaign
   (5) a resort hotel

19. Why was the Spartan way of life necessary?

   (1) to keep a hostile slave population under control
   (2) to fight off attacks from neighboring city-states
   (3) to insure success at the prestigious Olympic games
   (4) to please the gods and so live in Paradise
   (5) to survive in a land with few natural resources

PRACTICE TEST

Questions 20 and 21 refer to the following tax form and information.

Personal Allowances Worksheet

A Enter "1" for **yourself** if no one else can claim you as a dependent . . . . **A** _____

B Enter "1" if: {
- You are single and have only one job; or
- You are married, have only one job, and your spouse does not work; or
- Your wages from a second job or your spouse's wages (or the total of both) are $1,000 or less.
} . . **B** _____

C Enter "1" for your **spouse**. But, you may choose to enter -0- if you are married and have either a working spouse or more than one job. (Entering -0- may help you avoid having too little tax withheld.) . . . . **C** _____

D Enter number of **dependents** (other than your spouse or yourself) you will claim on your tax return . . . . **D** _____

E Enter "1" if you will file as **head of household** on your tax return (see conditions under **Head of household** above) . **E** _____

F Enter "1" if you have at least $1,500 of **child or dependent care expenses** for which you plan to claim a credit . . **F** _____

G **Child Tax Credit:**
- If your total income will be between $18,000 and $50,000 ($23,000 and $63,000 if married), enter "1" for each eligible child.
- If your total income will be between $50,000 and $80,000 ($63,000 and $115,000 if married), enter "1" if you have two eligible children, enter "2" if you have three or four eligible children, or enter "3" if you have five or more eligible children. **G** _____

H Add lines A through G and enter total here. Note: *This may be different from the number of exemptions you claim on your tax return.* ► **H** _____
Enter the number from line H on line 5 of Form W-4 below.

Form **W-4** | **Employee's Withholding Allowance Certificate** | **2000**
Department of the Treasury
Internal Revenue Service

| **1** Type or print your first name and middle initial | Last name | **2** Your social security number |

| Home address (number and street or rural route) | **3** ☐ Single ☐ Married ☐ Married, but withhold at higher Single rate.
Note: *If married, but legally separated, or spouse is a nonresident alien, check the Single box.* |

| City or town, state, and ZIP code | **4** If your last name differs from that on your social security card, check here. **You must call 1-800-772-1213 for a new card** . . . ► ☐ |

5 Total number of allowances you are claiming (from line H above) . . . . **5** _____

6 Additional amount, if any, you want withheld from each paycheck . . . . **6** $ _____

7 I claim exemption from withholding for 2000, and I certify that I meet **BOTH** of the following conditions for exemption:
- Last year I had a right to a refund of **ALL** Federal income tax withheld because I had **NO** tax liability **AND**
- This year I expect a refund of **ALL** Federal income tax withheld because I expect to have **NO** tax liability.
If you meet both conditions, write "EXEMPT" here . . . . ► **7** _____

Under penalties of perjury, I certify that I am entitled to the number of withholding allowances claimed on this certificate, or I am entitled to claim exempt status.
Employee's signature

Date

Marcia is a single parent of two children. Last year she had only one job. She earned $26,680 and had $2,135 in child care expenses. She will file as a head of household on her tax return and will not itemize deductions.

20. What number should appear on line G of the worksheet?

(1) 0
(2) 1
(3) 2
(4) 3
(5) 4

21. What is the reason for the Form W-4 tax form?

(1) to confuse citizens like Marcia so that they pay more taxes than they need to
(2) to assign the specific use for Marcia's taxes among the many needs of the government
(3) to find out how many people in the United States are in Marcia's income bracket
(4) to tell employees how much they need to reimburse their workers for tax expenses
(5) to determine the amount of taxes that should be taken out of Marcia's salary

PRACTICE TEST

Question 22 refers to the following passage.

Taxes can be classified in three ways:

- A progressive tax takes a larger fraction of income from high-income people than it does from low-income people.

- A regressive tax takes a larger fraction of income from low-income people than from high-income people.

- A proportional tax takes the same fraction of income from high- and low-income people.

22. People who are raising children may be eligible for the child tax credit, thus lowering their amount of taxable income. How would the child tax credit be classified?

   (1) It is somewhat regressive.
   (2) It is somewhat progressive.
   (3) The classification is proportional.
   (4) The classification depends on how many children a person has.
   (5) It has no effect on people's federal income tax.

Questions 23 and 24 refer to the following political cartoon.

23. This cartoon is by Thomas Nast, a German immigrant who was America's most famous editorial cartoonist in the nineteenth century. What view does Nast express in this cartoon?

   (1) We must place our trust in the principles of democracy.
   (2) America should remain a welcoming haven for immigrants.
   (3) Large corporations are forming trusts to undermine American free enterprise and competition.
   (4) There is so much fraud in American elections that the results cannot be trusted.
   (5) Pollution in New York's harbor has become worse and worse.

PRACTICE TEST

24. What might a twenty-first century version of this cartoon be?

(1) a stronger and taller Statue of Liberty draped with American flags
(2) the globe covered with trademark signs from multi-national corporations
(3) the Capitol building hugging the president and the Supreme Court
(4) a graph showing stock declines in the businesses noted in Nast's cartoon
(5) the same picture located in St. Peter's Square in Moscow, Russia

25. The Federal Reserve System controls the rate of growth in the money supply of the United States as a means of controlling both recession and inflation. In times of recession, the unemployment rate rises. In times of inflation, costs and prices rise, but there is no increase in productivity.

Which of the events listed below would probably result in the Federal Reserve tightening the money supply by increasing interest rates, thereby making money and credit less available?

(1) increase in unemployment rate
(2) decrease in corporate investment
(3) increase in birth rate
(4) decrease in consumer spending
(5) increase in the inflation rate

Questions 26 and 27 refer to the following bar graph.

Percent of Labor Force by Age Group, 1998 and projected 2008

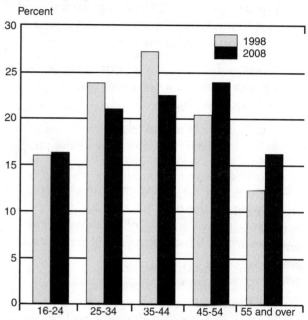

Source: Bureau of Labor Statistics

26. Which age group is expected to form the largest percent of the labor force in 2008?

(1) ages 16–24
(2) ages 25–35
(3) ages 35–44
(4) ages 45–54
(5) ages 55 and over

27. Which statement best summarizes the projected changes in the labor force in 2008?

(1) Older workers will make up a larger part of the labor force.
(2) The average age of workers will decrease.
(3) Little change is expected in the age distribution of the labor force.
(4) The size of the labor force will increase.
(5) There will be a slight increase in the 16–24 age group.

PRACTICE TEST

Questions 28 and 29 refer to the following passage.

The U.S. has the most technologically powerful, diverse, advanced, and largest economy in the world, with a per capita GDP [gross domestic product] of $33,900. In this market-oriented economy, private individuals and business firms make most of the decisions, and government obtains most of its goods and services in the private marketplace. U.S. business firms enjoy considerably greater flexibility than their counterparts in Western Europe and Japan in decisions to expand capital plants, lay off surplus workers, and develop new products. At the same time, they face higher barriers to entry in their rivals' home markets than the barriers to entry of foreign firms in U.S. markets. U.S. firms are at or near the forefront in technological advances, especially in computers and in medical, aerospace, and military equipment, although their advantage has narrowed since the end of World War II. The onrush of technology largely explains the gradual development of a "two-tier labor market" in which those at the bottom lack the education and the professional/technical skills of those at the top and, more and more, fail to get pay raises, health insurance coverage, and other benefits. Since 1975, practically all the gains in household income have gone to the top 20% of households.

–CIA World Factbook 2000

28. What is a method that countries use to restrict access to their markets?

    (1) sign free-trade agreements
    (2) flood foreign markets with inexpensive products
    (3) increase the productivity of local industries
    (4) put high taxes on imported goods
    (5) do away with quotas on goods from other countries

29. While the U.S. economy clearly is very strong, what does the author seem to assume is a problem?

    (1) an over-reliance on military spending
    (2) increasing income differences between the rich and the poor
    (3) excessive amounts of exports
    (4) government's need to make purchases in the private marketplace
    (5) lack of diversity in the goods and services available

Questions 30 and 31 refer to the following map.

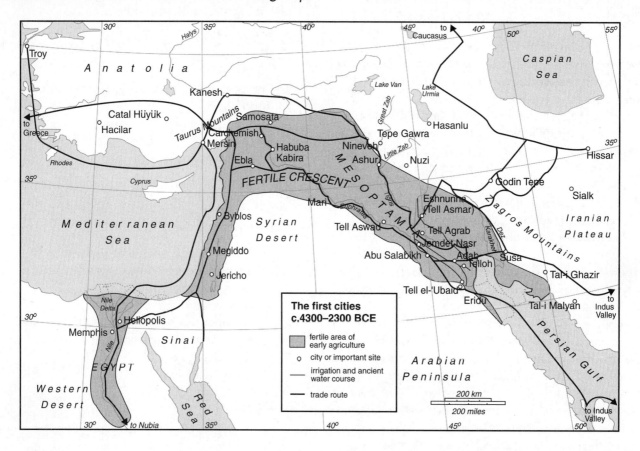

The first cities
c.4300–2300 BCE

- fertile area of early agriculture
- ○ city or important site
- — irrigation and ancient water course
- ━ trade route

200 km
200 miles

Farmers from northern and central Mesopotamia began to settle near the Tigris and Euphrates Rivers around 6000 B.C.E. (Before the Christian Era). Irrigation enabled enough food to be produced to support communities.

30. The map shows the Fertile Crescent where the first cities were built around 3500 B.C.E. In what part of the world did this happen?

(1) Central Africa
(2) Northern Europe
(3) Southern Europe
(4) Middle East
(5) South Africa

31. What made the development of these cities possible?

(1) one emperor ruling the entire area
(2) the invention of bronze
(3) agricultural improvements
(4) a religion that believed in a single god
(5) a family structure that promoted farming

PRACTICE TEST

Questions 32–35 refer to the following passage and map.

This map shows total water use in the United States in 1990, when about 408,000 million gallons of water were used each day (Mgal/d). California used the most water, about 46,800 Mgal/d, with most of that going for irrigation. Texas had the second highest water use, about 25,200 Mgal/d, mostly for use in the power-production industries and for irrigation.

Total Water Withdrawals in the United States in 1990

Legend:
- 0 – 2,000
- 2,000 – 5,000
- 5,000 – 10,000
- 10,000 – 20,000
- 20,000 – 48,000

(Million gallons per day)

Source: U.S. Geologic Service

32. Which region of the United States seemed to use the fewest million gallons of water?

   (1) the Pacific Northwest
   (2) the Deep South
   (3) northern New England
   (4) the Southwest
   (5) the Mid-Atlantic

33. What was most of the water in Florida probably used for?

   (1) irrigation
   (2) residences
   (3) industrial plants
   (4) air-conditioning
   (5) generating electricity

34. Which of these states used more water than did the states surrounding it?

   (1) Pennsylvania
   (2) South Dakota
   (3) Indiana
   (4) Idaho
   (5) Georgia

35. Which of the following facts about California probably explains best why it used more water than any other state?

   (1) It has the greatest land area of any state.
   (2) It is a major producer of fruits and vegetables.
   (3) It is prone to earthquakes and other seismic disturbances.
   (4) It has a wide variety of terrains.
   (5) It has a rapidly growing population.

PRACTICE TEST

Questions 36–39 refer to the following chart about the government of the United States.

THE GOVERNMENT OF THE UNITED STATES

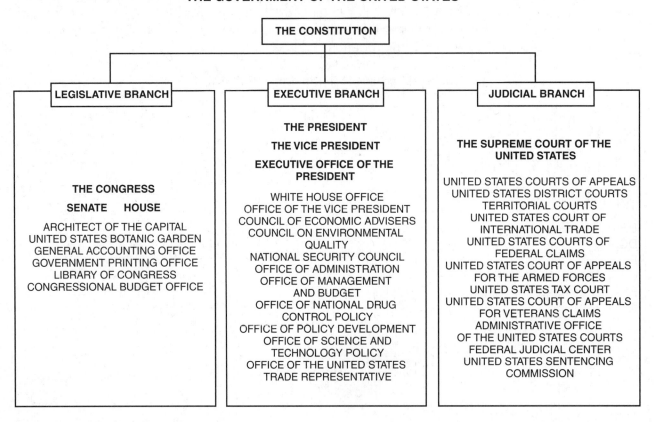

36. According to the chart, which of the following is part of the legislative branch of the government?

    (1) General Accounting Office
    (2) Council of Economic Advisers
    (3) Office of Management and Budget
    (4) National Security Council
    (5) United States Tax Court

37. From this chart, it is possible to determine which of the following?

    (1) The U.S. Congress can impeach the President.
    (2) Convicted criminals can be pardoned by a state governor.
    (3) National security is the responsibility of the President.
    (4) The Congress can declare war on another nation.
    (5) The President appoints judges to the Supreme Court.

38. The top box on this chart is labeled "The Constitution." What underlying principle of the Constitution is most clearly illustrated by the chart?

    (1) reserved powers
    (2) separation of powers
    (3) federalism
    (4) domestic tranquility
    (5) concurrent powers

39. What is the main purpose of this chart?

    (1) to explain the responsibilities of each branch of government
    (2) to demonstrate how the system of checks and balances works
    (3) to show how the government is structured
    (4) to list all the major government agencies
    (5) to distinguish between elected and appointed government positions

PRACTICE TEST

Questions 40 and 41 refer to the following table.

Persons Reported Registered and Voted by Selected States: 1996

State	Voting-age population (1,000)	Percent of voting-age population	
		Registered	Voted
U.S.	193,651 Total	65.9 Ave.	54.2 Ave.
AL	3,139	73.8	55.6
AK	404	75.7	59.5
AZ	3,149	58.5	47.3
AR	1,843	64.4	51.5
CA	22,871	56.1	48.4
CO	2,859	70.0	58.8
CT	2,409	69.9	58.5
DE	536	64.0	54.7
DC	402	73.0	59.6
FL	10,886	61.8	50.7
GA	5,303	66.1	49.6
HI	839	55.1	43.1
ID	835	68.4	60.1
IL	8,598	67.7	55.6
IN	4,238	68.5	55.8
IA	2,113	73.0	61.1
KS	1,823	68.9	62.0
KY	2,906	69.4	52.8
LA	3,098	73.4	61.8
ME	926	81.5	67.7
MD	3,766	65.9	54.4
MA	4,560	66.7	56.3
MI	7,018	72.0	58.1
MN	3,375	78.3	66.9

Source: U.S. Census Bureau

40. Which of these states was above the national average in the percent of people registered but below the national average in the percent who actually voted?

(1) Alabama
(2) California
(3) Delaware
(4) Georgia
(5) Minnesota

41. Which of these states had the highest percent of people who were registered AND voted in 1996?

(1) Arkansas
(2) Colorado
(3) Iowa
(4) Kansas
(5) Minnesota

Question 42 refers to the following quotation from Alexis de Tocqueville's Democracy in America.

"The electors see their representative not only as a legislator for the state but also as the natural protector of local interests in the legislature; indeed, they almost seem to think that he has a power of attorney to represent each constituent, and they trust him to be as eager in their private interests as in those of the country."

42. Which of these actions by a member of the House of Representatives most clearly illustrates de Tocqueville's point?

(1) voting to pass the president's program
(2) attending committee hearings and asking questions
(3) working to avoid the closing of a military base in the district
(4) inserting a speech in the *Congressional Record*
(5) sending a newsletter to constituents to explain his or her voting record

PRACTICE TEST

Questions 43 and 44 refer to the following map about adult illiteracy.

Adult Illiteracy Rate 1995

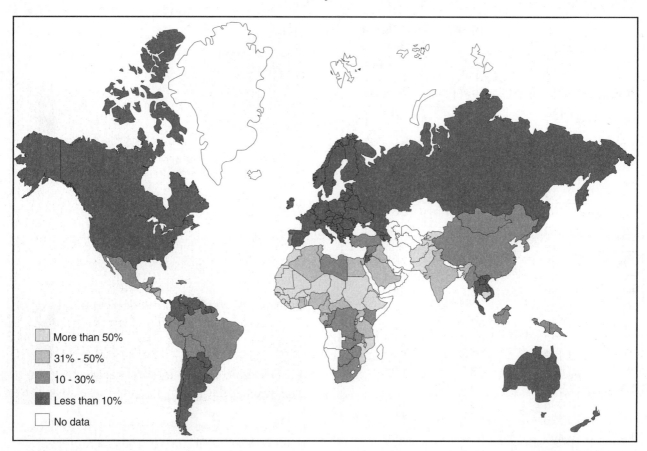

More than 50%

31% - 50%

10 - 30%

Less than 10%

No data

Source: UN Basic Social Services

43. Which of the following has an adult illiteracy rate similar to that of Australia?

(1) Africa
(2) Central America
(3) Southern Asia
(4) South America
(5) Western Europe

44. Which of the following is *not* a conclusion that follows logically from the information in the map?

(1) A lot of financial and instructional resources are being given by the dark colored countries to address illiteracy in the lighter countries.

(2) People in the darkest-shaded countries on the map probably have higher standards of living than those in the more lightly-shaded countries.

(3) The reason that so many countries in Africa struggle with the problem of illiteracy may be connected to their history of European colonialism.

(4) War and political upheaval are likely reasons that we don't have information about illiteracy in much of the Middle East and Central Asia.

(5) Most of the world's military and economic power lie in countries where there is a well-supported and highly structured system of education.

PRACTICE TEST

Question 45 refers to the following chart about South America.

GDP and Illiteracy in South America

Country	GDP Per Capita (US$, 1997)	Adult Illiteracy Rate (%, 1995) Total
Argentina	9070	3.6
Brazil	4930	16.8
Chile	5271	5.1
Colombia	2384	9.6
Ecuador	1648	9.9
Peru	2674	12
Venezuela	3678	8.5

Source: UN Statistics

45. Which nation listed in the chart combines a relatively high gross domestic product (GDP) per capita with a high adult illiteracy rate?

(1) Argentina
(2) Brazil
(3) Chile
(4) Colombia
(5) Ecuador

Question 46 refers to the following photograph.

46. The photograph shows a crowd of 250,000 people listening to Dr. Martin Luther King, Jr.'s "I have a dream" speech on August 28, 1963. What fundamental principle of American political life does this photograph illustrate?

(1) By engaging in civil disobedience, demonstrators appeal to the conscience of the nation.
(2) The First Amendment guarantees the right of people to assemble and speak.
(3) The two major political parties are the primary organizers of American political life.
(4) State governments have some powers that are concurrent with the powers of the national government.
(5) The Founders wanted an absolute wall of separation between Church and State.

PRACTICE TEST

Questions 47 and 48 refer to the following document.

In a criminal case, all jurors must agree on a verdict. In a civil case, the instruction of the court will state how many must agree. Jurors must enter the discussion with an open mind. They should exchange views freely and should not hesitate to change opinions. Jurors have a duty to give full consideration to the opinion of their fellow jurors. They should try to reach a verdict whenever possible. No juror is required to give up any opinion which that juror is convinced is correct.

Under most circumstances, jurors need not tell anyone how the jury arrived at the verdict. A disclosure is required only if a judge orders a juror to reveal such matters. To decide cases fairly, jurors must be honest, intelligent and have both integrity and judgment.

To meet their responsibility, jurors must decide the facts and apply the law impartially. They must not favor either the rich or the poor. They must treat all men and women, corporations and individuals alike. Justice should be given to all persons without regard to race, national origin, creed, color or sex.

—from The State Bar of South Dakota

47. What is one important message in this document?

(1) to persuade jurors to get along with other jurors
(2) to be sure jurors follow the lead of the foreperson
(3) to honor all the obligations of citizenship
(4) to make judgments without prejudice
(5) to give the defendant the benefit of the doubt

48. Which of the following behaviors is NOT permitted?

(1) having a different opinion than all the other jurors in a criminal case and refusing to go along with the majority
(2) changing one's mind during the course of deliberations after listening to one of the other jurors
(3) giving up on trying to reach a verdict after lengthy discussions
(4) revealing how the jury arrived at a verdict when the judge orders such disclosure
(5) deciding to award damages in a civil case because the plaintiff is poor and the defendant is rich

Question 49 refers to the following line graph.

Demand Curve

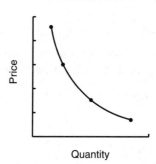

49. The curve in the graph shows the demand curve. According to the law of downward-sloping demand, what happens when the price of a good is raised?

(1) More people will buy the good.
(2) The quality of the good decreases.
(3) Fewer producers will supply the good.
(4) Fewer people will buy the good.
(5) Consumers will boycott the good.

PRACTICE TEST

Question 50 refers to the following political cartoon.

—From *Herblock: A Cartoonist's Life* (Times Books, 1998)

50. What is the main idea of this cartoon?

(1) Prayer should be allowed in government buildings.
(2) Members of Congress aren't serious about changing how political campaigns are financed.
(3) The people of the United States should march on the Capitol to demand campaign-funding reform.
(4) Challengers have little chance of unseating incumbent members of Congress without a reform of campaign funding.
(5) Citizens should pray for their representatives in Congress.

Answer Key

1. **(3)** This section lists the grievances the colonists have against the king in order to justify their formation of a new government.

2. **(2)** Tyranny conveys the idea of cruel and despotic power; absolute makes the phrase even stronger. All the other phrases are more objective in tone.

3. **(3)** The colonists feared executive power such as that held by the king. They believed that the system of checks and balances would keep any branch of government from having too much power.

4. **(1)** The phrase suggests the strength of the colonists' opposition to the king.

5. **(5)** Southerners wanted the Fugitive Slave Law strengthened. All the other provisions were ones the North wanted.

6. **(1)** By looking at the map, you can see that the area in question is located in the West, not in northern cities or Canada. Railroad expansion came later, and the war in Mexico happened earlier.

7. **(4)** The figure represents the United States, as shown by his costume and the fact that he is sitting apart from the European powers.

8. **(2)** If China had been powerful and independent, it wouldn't have been "up for grabs" to the imperial nations at the time.

9. **(1)** The European powers are shown dividing up a huge cake, while the U.S. gets only a small cupcake. This indicates the cartoonist's view that U.S. imperialism is a small matter. The caption reinforces this point.

10. **(3)** Washington stresses the importance of enlightened public opinion, which is improved by education. While not envisioned by Washington, public universities serve this function. Censorship, the railroads, and sectional differences do not.

11. **(3)** The graphs clearly show that the North had an overwhelming advantage in material and a substantial advantage in men.

12. **(4)** The bar for third parties is by far the highest for 1992. Also, in this year neither candidate got a majority of the vote.

13. **(5)** The graph does not indicate any of the options except the last one. The dark bars in the graph, representing the Democrats, steadily increase in height between 1980 and 1996.

14. **(4)** Like the Constitutional Convention, at which representatives from the various states gathered to organize their government and then seek approval from the states themselves, the countries of the proposed United Nations worked together to define the purpose and activities of their organization and then sought support from within each nation.

15. **(4)** The Dumbarton Oaks meeting was held in 1944 when World War II was going on. Germany was the enemy of the United States, China, the United Kingdom, and the Soviet Union, and so would not have been invited to the conference.

16. **(3)** The fall of the Berlin Wall was cause to celebrate democracy (1), the will of the people (2), the end to the Cold War (4), and a reunified Germany (5). There would be no cause, however, to salute the Soviets, since it was the Soviet claim on East Germany that was ending.

17. **(2)** The text states that *helot* was the name given to a slave.

18. **(3)** Spartan conditions would be found in an army barracks where there is little in the way of comfort or luxury. All the other institutions would be more comfortable.

PRACTICE TEST

19. (1) The text states that it was the need to keep the slaves under control that led to the Spartan way of life.

20. (3) Because Marcia's income is less than $50,000, she is to fill in the blank with the number of children she has: 2.

21. (5) The sole purpose of this document is to calculate how much of Marcia's salary should be withdrawn by the government as taxes.

22. (2) For a lower-income group, this credit will lessen the fraction of income to which the tax applies, so it has a progressive effect on the income tax.

23. (3) Nast was concerned about companies combining in trusts and controlling American competition. The cartoon is directed against these companies. It does not concern immigrants, elections, or pollution.

24. (2) Large corporations are now dominating the entire world in the same way they did the United States in the mid-to late 1800s. The dominance of companies such as Coca-Cola and McDonalds in many countries makes it difficult for local businesses to develop and succeed.

25. (5) When the inflation rate increases, the Federal Reserve tends to tighten the money supply in order to avoid recession. Increases in unemployment and decreases in business investment and in consumer spending have the opposite effect. Changes in the birth rate, though they can affect the economy, are irrelevant here.

26. (4) The tallest black bar (2008) represents the 45–54 age group. All other age groups have shorter black bars, indicating each makes up a smaller percentage of the 2008 workforce.

27. (1) The graph shows that there will be a significant change because the number of older workers will increase.

28. (4) High tariffs are a barrier to trade. They increase the cost of the imported goods and protect domestic goods. Joining trade agreements, improving productivity, and lifting quotas all serve to increase trade.

29. (2) In the last sentence of the text, the point is made that income difference between the rich and the poor is a problem.

30. (4) This area is located along rivers in the Middle East. The area is now located in Syria, Iraq, Israel, and Egypt. All the other locations are incorrect.

31. (3) Agricultural improvements, specifically irrigation, led to the development of cities. Because there was a surplus of food, everyone did not have to farm in order to be fed.

32. (3) The lightest color is northern New England, so this area must use the least water.

33. (1) The text points out the use of water for irrigation in California, and it seems likely that the same thing is true in Florida, a major producer of agricultural products.

34. (4) Idaho is a darker color than the states that surround it, indicating that it uses more water.

35. (2) The fact that California is a major producer of fruits and vegetables explains why so much water is needed for irrigation. While population is important, the text underscores the use of irrigation.

36. (1) Of these, only the General Accounting Office appears in the Legislative section of the chart.

37. (3) While all of the statement are true, the chart only gives information to support the choice concerning responsibility for national security.

38. (2) The chart's division into three sections shows the separation of powers among different branches of the government. Reserved powers belong to the states and concurrent powers are shared with the states.

39. (3) This chart simply shows the structure of the government. It does not explain anything, nor does it list all the agencies.

40. (4) Georgia had 66.1% of its voters register, above the national average of 65.9%, but only 49.6% voted—below the national average of 54.2%.

41. (5) Minnesota had 78.3% of its voting age population registered and 66.9% voted.

42. (3) When a representative works to prevent a base closing, he is closely serving local interests.

43. (5) If you compare the shading for Australia, you will see that it is the same as that for Western Europe.

44. (1) The other choices could follow logically, given the information in the map.

45. (2) Brazil has the highest illiteracy rate (16.8%) and the third highest GDP, behind Argentina and Chile.

46. (2) Events such as the March on Washington, August 28, 1963, depend on the First Amendment guarantees. This photo does not show civil disobedience or political parties.

47. (4) The text repeatedly emphasizes the importance of treating all people alike and of deciding based on the evidence. Jurors need not get along with fellow jurors or follow the lead of the foreperson. The text focuses on jury duty, not other aspects of citizenship. There is no mention of the benefit of the doubt.

48. (5) The document specifically states the jurors must not favor either the rich or the poor. Jurors are encouraged to hold onto their opinion and, if appropriate, to change their minds during deliberation. They are told to follow the judge's orders on disclosure and to reach a verdict only if it is possible.

49. (4) An important economic principle is that when the price of a good goes up, demand for that good goes down. In other words, fewer people will buy the good. If the price goes down, more people will buy the good.

50. (2) The phrase *lip service* suggests a lack of seriousness. The cartoonist indicates that members of Congress are not serious about reform.

Evaluation Chart

Below and on page 132 are two Evaluation Charts. Use the chart below **if you want to concentrate on Social Studies subject areas.** Use the chart on page 132 **if you want to concentrate on Social Studies themes.** Circle the number of any question you answered incorrectly. If you need extra help with some of the skills, content areas, or themes, turn to those sections in Contemporary's *GED Social Studies* or *Complete GED.*

Skill Area Content Area	Comprehension (S*: 27–42) (C*: 217–230)	Application (S: 43–58) (C: 231–236)	Analysis (S: 59–98) (C: 237–262)	Evaluation (S: 99–115) (C: 271–274)
U.S. History (S: 119–156, 183–215) (C: 327–366)	7, 11, 12	5, 10	1, 2, 3, 4, 6, 9, 13	
World History (S: 119–156, 283–326) (C: 297–326)	17, 19	15, 18	8, 14	16
Geography (S: 157–181) (C: 427–443)	32, 34, 43	30, 33, 35	31, 45	44
Economics (S: 217–251) (C: 399–426)	26	20, 28, 49	21, 22, 23, 27	24, 25, 29
Civics and Government (S: 183–215) (C: 367–398)	36, 39, 40, 41, 50	42, 46, 48		37, 38, 47

* S =Contemporary's *GED Social Studies*
  C =Contemporary's *Complete GED*

Evaluation Chart

Skill Area/ Content Area	Comprehension (S*: 27–42) (C*: 217–230)	Application (S: 43–58) (C: 231–236)	Analysis (S: 59–98) (C: 237–262)	Evaluation (S: 99–115) (C: 271–274)
Time, Continuity, and Change (S*: 119–156)	17, 19	18		16
Places and People (S: 157–181)	32, 34	30, 33, 35	31	
Power, Authority, and Governance (S: 183–215)	12, 36, 39, 40, 41, 50	5, 10, 42, 46, 48	1, 2, 3, 4, 6, 13	37, 38, 47
Production, Distribution, and Consumption (S: 217–251)	11, 26	20, 49	21, 22, 23, 27	24, 25
Science, Technology, and Society (S: 253–282)		28		29
Global Connections (S: 283–326)	7, 43	15	8, 9, 14, 45	44

* S =Contemporary's *GED Social Studies*
  C=Contemporary's *Complete GED*

Answer Key

Time, Continuity, and Change, pages 3–20

1. (3) **Comprehension** Florida was outside the area outlined as the United States in 1783; it was admitted as a state in 1846.

2. (2) **Comprehension** California is shown within the borders of the territory acquired in the Mexican Cession.

3. (2) **Analysis** Following the Louisiana Purchase, greater expanses of territory were annexed. None of the other choices can be supported by information in this map.

4. (1) **Application** The Niagara Movement preceded the NAACP and sought an end to discriminatory practices based on race.

5. (2) **Application** Both the American Missionary Association and the Peace Corps relied on volunteers who were willing to leave their homes to help others in need.

6. (5) **Analysis** The statement that Americans of the 1930s were "a more formidable breed" is an opinion that is signaled in the passage by the word "think." All of the other choices are facts.

7. (5) **Analysis** The first paragraph states that the Depression followed the stock-market crash of October 1929. This shows that the stock-market crash was a cause of the Depression.

8. (5) **Analysis** The last paragraph contains the sentence "The others I've interviewed wonder as well." This is a clue that the writer was surveying people from the Depression years. None of the other choices can be supported by the evidence.

9. (5) **Comprehension** Dellie Norton describes the impact of the Depression on Appalachia this way: "Prosperity went instantly from little to none." In other words, Appalachia frequently suffered economic hardship.

10. (1) **Evaluation** The author introduces the editorial by referring to the "media's intrusion into a politician's personal life for the entertainment value it offers." This statement is critical of the media. None of the other choices is supported by the information in the passage.

11. (2) **Analysis** The editorial focuses on the sensationalism of media and assumes that selling newspapers and increasing ratings are more important to the media than reporting the facts.

12. (5) **Analysis** By stating "By and large, the American people want to be entertained—not informed" and by referring to the sales figures of certain tabloids, the writer is presenting the opinion that the media are only giving the people what they want.

13. (2) **Evaluation** Choice (2) is the only situation that compares a private citizen's behavior to that of a candidate or a politician in office.

14. (3) **Evaluation** The editorial makes no claim about the standards of conduct that should be expected of presidents; it focuses only on the media's reporting about politicians' personal lives. Choices (1), (2), (4), and (5) all are either stated or implied in the editorial.

15. (3) **Comprehension** When the authors refer to the difficulty of finding pediatricians, arranging repair appointments, and making child-care arrangements, they are suggesting that society has not made adjustments to provide for the increase in the number of working mothers.

16. (5) **Analysis** The statement that "the bottom line of the message remains clear to anyone who has lived through it—the normal mother, the caring mother, the good mother, is at home" suggests society still believes that because they hold jobs, working mothers are not normal, caring, or as good as mothers who stay home to raise their children.

17. (2) **Analysis** According to the chart, the year 1933 had the lowest GNP, level of personal income, and consumer price index, and the highest unemployment rate.

18. (2) **Evaluation** According to the chart, in 1941 GNP and personal income were up, and unemployment was down. The economy was stronger than it had been in previous years, so you can infer that America's involvement in the war led to a stronger economy.

19. (2) **Evaluation** The only answer that reasonably explains the low unemployment rate achieved between 1941 and 1945 is that factories at peak production capacity for the war effort had to hire many workers. None of the other choices alone can fully explain the increase in employment.

20. (2) **Analysis** According to the facts in the chart, the CPI for the 1930s and 1940s was between $40 and $50, compared to $100 for 1967 (the chart states under CPI that 1967=100). This is roughly half the CPI of 1967 ($100). There is no data in the chart for the year 2001.

21. (3) **Comprehension** The passage states that before Levittown, only the rich and upper-middle class could afford houses in suburbia. The houses were built for returning servicemen who would be seeking jobs after the war. It is unlikely that the poverty-stricken or the wealthy would have been potential buyers of the houses.

22. (2) **Application** Forbidding African Americans to buy houses in Levittown would have violated the Housing Act of 1968, which outlawed racial discrimination in federally financed housing. None of the other choices involves discrimination in housing.

23. (1) **Comprehension** Distance from the city is the only disadvantage of living in the suburbs that is not cited in the passage.

24. (2) **Comprehension** According to the passage, many laborers moved to Chicago for jobs but lost them when construction decreased. Unions were formed when the laborers began to lose their jobs.

25. (3) **Analysis** The only opinion among the choices is that Chicago was exciting but unglamorous. The other choices are facts that can be proved.

26. (1) **Evaluation** The NAFTA agreement creating a free-trade zone along the border is the most reasonable hypothesis to explain the explosive growth throughout the region. The drug war and illegal immigration problems have been deterrents to growth. There is no evidence that would indicate anything about the quality of life or any imminent collapse.

27. (5) **Evaluation** The rapid growth along the border during the past decade is strong evidence that the trend will continue through the next decade. No evidence is given to support the other predictions.

28. (4) **Analysis** The writer states that "Grownups know that little things matter." She then goes on to describe the insults and humiliations piled on Jeffords by the White House staff. It is clear that the author considered this behavior both arrogant and immature.

29. (4) **Analysis** Since party changes are so rare, just by announcing his shift, Jeffords was able to define President George W. Bush as ignoring moderates and catering to conservatives. He did not outline his poor treatment at the hands of the Republican leadership; the author of the passage did that.

30. (3) **Comprehension** The passage paints a negative picture of the overall situation in Russia, pointing out its political and economic shortcomings.

31. (1) **Analysis** The breakup of the Soviet dictatorship provided a great opportunity for Russia. The other four choices are all reasons why that opportunity was squandered.

32. (2) **Analysis** Underlying much of the economic mismanagement of Russia is a high level of political corruption. Examples given in the passage include insider privatization and punitive and arbitrary taxation. The passage also states that the civil bureaucracy and armed forces have not been reformed. Of the choices given, reducing corruption in government would have the greatest impact on improving conditions in Russia.

33. (1) **Analysis** In his statement, Henry N. Tisdale describes the importance of historical artifacts and books on black campuses. Therefore, he would most likely think that preserving these things would be most important.

34. (1) **Application** Just as some colleges have historically been for African Americans, women's colleges are important as sources of artifacts, books, and history for the women's movement in America.

35. (4) **Analysis** The greatest imbalance in Americans' moving from one region to the other occurs between the Northeast and the South. While 405,000 people moved from the Northeast to the South, only 183,000 moved to the Northeast from the South, an imbalance of 222,000 people.

36. (2) **Analysis** The warm weather in the South, especially in Florida, is the most likely reason that so many people have moved there. While there are technology companies in the South, it is not known for being a center of technology (1) or for having a larger number of job openings than other parts of the country (4). While the South is known for its hospitality and beauty (3), that alone is probably not the reason so many people moved there. The South does have some large cities, but none of the three largest cities in the country are located in the South (5).

37. (1) **Comprehension** From 1996 to 2000, on average, murder decreased the most, 6.6% per year. All the other types of violent crime decreased less than 5% per year.

38. (5) **Comprehension** From 1996 to 2000, violent crime decreased in all categories. In 2000, there was a slight 0.1% increase.

39. (3) **Evaluation** There is no evidence in either the graph or the maps that growth will dramatically slow down or that Las Vegas is facing an economic downturn. The maps show that the developed area of Las Vegas has rapidly spread, with no evidence of any possibility of controls on sprawl or new development. With Los Angeles presently the largest city in the Western United States, it is unlikely that Las Vegas will ever be the largest city in the West. It is most likely that growth and development in Las Vegas will continue in the near future.

40. (5) **Evaluation** Las Vegas is located in an extremely hot and dry area in southern Nevada. The entire Southwestern United States faces a shortage of water. Therefore, Las Vegas's greatest challenge will be finding sufficient supplies of water.

41. (5) **Analysis** Unemployment insurance has turned out to be extremely popular in the United States. The idea was originally proposed by the Socialist Party. The popularity of the idea makes it least likely that it was a cause of the decline of the Socialist Party in the United States.

42. (1) **Application** Since Bebel and Kautsky expected socialism to triumph in the United States, they would have been least surprised by the success of Roosevelt's New Deal, which implemented much of the Socialist Party's agenda. All of the other choices describe conservative developments, which ran contrary to Bebel and Kautsky's predictions.

43. (2) **Analysis** The painting American Gothic depicts a typical American farming couple. By using this composition, but replacing the couple with an Asian American and an African American, the cartoonist is trying to convey that typical Americans can be of Asian or African descent as well as European.

44. (3) **Analysis** If the observers had been aware of the harmful effects of radiation, they would not have been observing the atom bomb blast without protection.

45. (4) **Analysis** In the early 1950s, the United States government would most likely have wanted to maintain popular support for the atomic bomb testing program. The passage does not provide support for any of the other choices.

46. (5) **Comprehension** The passage points to many industries over more than one hundred years that have followed similar patterns of growth. The main point that the author is trying to make is that what is happening to Internet companies is following that pattern.

47. (1) **Analysis** Although we cannot know for sure which companies will survive the current downturn, the information in the article presents a convincing argument that some major Internet companies will survive.

48. (3) **Analysis** This well-known painting openly glorifies those who participated in the revolution and promotes American nationalism.

49. (2) **Comprehension** The picture shows beautiful public buildings in the foreground with ugly industrial sprawl in the background. The passage contrasts the ugliness of the new urban centers with the grand public buildings.

50. (4) **Analysis** The builders of Birmingham's public buildings were probably unaware of the long term impact of air pollution to their buildings. Although they may not have cared about the workers, they probably had some awareness of their difficult lives, at least through the fiction of Charles Dickens.

Places and People, pages 21–36

1. (4) **Comprehension** The summarizing sentence, "It was the first deed of Indian land to English colonists," is a clue that Samoset was an Indian or Native American leader.

2. (3) **Evaluation** The facts that Manhattan Island was bought for so little and that Samoset believed that land came from the Great Spirit both suggest that the Native Americans did not perceive land as having monetary value.

3. (2) **Application** In general, Americans believe that everything material has its price; therefore, the purchase of Manhattan Island and the deeding of Pemaquid land demonstrate this belief. None of the other answer choices is supported by the facts stated in the question.

4. (2) **Analysis** All of the choices except choice (2) contain a reasonable conclusion that follows from the premise. The statement that the Great Spirit provides land is unrelated to the conclusion that land is endless.

5. (1) **Comprehension** According to the map's key, Alaska had a ratio of between 101 and 150 doctors per 100,000 people.

6. (4) **Analysis** Four out of the six states with a ratio of 200–299 doctors per 100,000 people—New York, Massachusetts, Connecticut, and Maryland—are located in the Northeast and are urban and industrial.

7. (4) **Analysis** The map gives no information regarding the population of the states (2), their need for doctors (1) and (5), or the health status of their residents (3). The statement about medical schools and hospitals is the only possible choice because it uses sound logic together with the word may and makes no assumptions about information that is not provided by the map.

8. (2) **Analysis** Climate does not contribute directly to the number of doctors in an area. Each of the other factors does.

9. (1) **Evaluation** The last sentence of the passage refers to cultural features—art, politics, manners, religion, and industry—as being affected by the Pacific. This suggests that the development of a culture is influenced by the natural environment in which it grows.

10. (5) **Analysis** The passage tells us that Pacific Islanders have little desire to master other men, one of the primary causes of wars.

11. (5) **Analysis** The cartoon depicts big-energy businesses as they prepare to bat at Earth, with the approval of the White House. The businesses are presented as immature and irresponsible children, meaning that Earth is at risk in their hands. Therefore, the viewer can interpret the cartoonist's view as critical of the White House policy and concerned about its negative implications for the environment.

12. (1) **Application** Oil, coal, and nukes—the children playing in the cartoon—are all examples of big businesses involved in energy production. Although the auto and steel industries are big, they are not energy producers. Although solar and thermal represent energy sources, they are not big businesses. Only gas is an example of a business that is both big and focused on energy.

13. (5) **Comprehension** According to the map's key, the darkest areas are the most humid. The largest dark area is located near the equator (0 degrees latitude), both north and south.

14. (2) **Comprehension** A greater number of dark areas (areas of high humidity) can be found along the east coast than along the west coast. Therefore, the west coast can be described as less humid.

15. (2) **Analysis** In the last sentence the writer emphasizes the professions of German Jews as a characteristic that distinguished them from the other Jewish groups. We can infer, therefore, that the other groups were not usually professionals such as doctors or lawyers.

16. (1) **Analysis** The second sentence suggests that devout Zionists did not assimilate into the German culture.

17. (4) **Analysis** Because German Jews, who were fully assimilated, or integrated, into the German society are contrasted with those Jews who were not, we can infer that a ghetto is a community that has not integrated into the larger society.

18. (5) **Application** Movements by an army would be shown on a map that depicts borders between counties, states, or territories—a political map.

19. (2) **Application** A population map describes the distribution of the population of an area. Minority representation refers to population distribution.

20. (4) **Application** The annual snowfall of a region relates to the weather and would be shown on a weather map.

21. (1) **Application** A topographical map would indicate features of the terrain, which would help a person unfamiliar with the land. None of the other maps would be useful to a soldier in helping him find his way around unfamiliar territory.

22. (4) **Comprehension** Cropland is the same as cultivated land. When compared to the region of the United States east of the Rocky Mountains, the West has relatively little tillable land.

23. (1) **Comprehension** According to the map, tundra land is shown only in the far northern areas.

24. (1) **Analysis** According to the map, a great percentage of the land in northern Canada is forested. Forests are sources of lumber.

25. (5) **Analysis** The purpose of the chart is to identify what kinds of jobs Chicanos had in 1930. A Chicano is someone who comes from Mexico. The greatest number of Chicanos would be concentrated in the area closest to Mexico. An analysis of large numbers by percent is much more revealing than an analysis of small numbers.

26. (4) **Comprehension** The columns on the far right of the chart list the percentages for the region overall. The largest percent under "F" (female) is in the service category (38.4).

27. (4) **Analysis** Of the countries listed, only Bermuda and the Netherlands Antilles are still European colonies (1). The Bahamas are part of the British Commonwealth, and the other countries mentioned are currently independent. None of the countries mentioned is located in the Indian Ocean (3); Guinea Bissau is in Africa on the Atlantic Coast, and the other countries are in or on the Caribbean. There is no mention in the article of whether the countries have accepted toxic waste from the United States (2) or imported fertilizer (5).

28. (1) **Evaluation** Given the description of the extremes to which the boat and its company went to get rid of the waste, it is unlikely that the company would clean up the mess it left. The other statements describe logical possibilities.

29. (3) **Application** Because the Khian Sea was dumping hazardous materials off on poorer countries and lying about what they really were in order to get rid of them, the incident is most similar to the company trying to sell defective parts at a lower price and lying about the quality of the parts in order to get rid of them.

30. (3) **Analysis** The U.S. government is responsible because of the looseness of its laws, which allows such waste to leave the country. The boat's owner is responsible because he contracted to do the dumping and directed the actions of the boat's crew, who carried out his orders. Large corporations are responsible because they produce much of the waste and want to be able to dispose of it as inexpensively as possible. Only the residents of Gonaïves, as the victims of the incident, are not at least partially responsible for what happened.

31. (3) **Analysis** Suburban housing tracts like these indicate a similar socioeconomic level in their residents. Since the houses are all the same, people who earn approximately the same amount of money buy and live in them.

32. (2) **Comprehension** The graph shows that not only was the sharpest increase in suburban land area in the South but also that Southern suburbs were spread over more square miles than suburbs in any other region.

33. (5) **Comprehension** The chart reports continued increases in growth in all regions, although in every place but the Midwest the growth rate slowed between 1990 and 2000. The region where it slowed the most dramatically was the West.

34. (5) **Application** Beauregard would have been called a scalawag because he supported the efforts of the North to rebuild the South after the war.

35. (4) **Application** The term carpetbagger was applied to Northerners who moved to the South in search of fortunes immediately after the Civil War.

36. (1) **Application** Since the Underground Railroad was a movement that helped slaves to reach freedom, it was a movement in which many abolitionists participated.

37. (5) **Application** Southern whites who had little to gain financially from the Reconstruction, but who still supported it, were called scalawags.

38. (3) **Analysis** Since the common aspect of both prison models was enforced silence, the novel element of the Auburn model was work. It can be inferred that prison reformers perceived that the two advantages to requiring prisoners to work rather than to simply sit alone and idle all day was the practical aspect of helping to maintain the prison, together with the development of discipline and focus, both considered positive qualities.

39. (3) **Application** There is no reference to educational opportunities for prisoners in either of the policies forwarded in the late 1800s. However, the other statements can be traced to either the solitary confinement model or the work model, both of which stressed silence, restriction, and reflection.

40. (4) **Evaluation** Since the picture shows prisoners doing unpleasant and physically demanding work, it could have been used to reassure anyone who thought that allowing prisoners some release from solitary confinement might be too "soft" an approach to reform. The image of prisoners toiling in a quarry is hardly a vision of an easy existence.

41. (2) **Comprehension** In the portion of the flyer about paper, the flyer states that no gift wrap is to be included among the materials left for recycling.

42. (5) **Application** Environmentalists are people who are concerned about the environment and the impact that human beings have upon it. Recycling is an activity that is considered helpful to the environment because it prevents the dumping of materials that decompose slowly and instead finds ways for them to be used again. None of the other groups are known for a particular stance on recycling or environmental issues.

43. (3) **Comprehension** Near the beginning of the speech, Lincoln states to the audience that "we are engaged in a great civil war" and that "we are met on a great battle-field of that war."

44. (1) **Comprehension** Toward the end of the speech Lincoln eloquently urges people to take "increased devotion to that cause" for which the soldiers at Gettysburg gave up their lives: to prevent this country from perishing.

45. (3) **Comprehension** Kansas is in the interior of the United States and is far from any ocean. An ocean view in Kansas would indicate a drastic amount of melting of the polar ice caps, a direct and extremely serious effect of global warming.

46. (4) **Analysis** The last paragraph of the passage refers to the older people in the camps who remember with nostalgia where they came from and how much better their living conditions were in their original homes. This same passage contradicts statement choice (1): clearly the Palestinians have not lived in Gaza for centuries but rather for only a few decades. Political organization, choice (2), is not mentioned. The map showing Gaza's proximity to the Mediterranean Sea contradicts statement (3) and the tone in the reference to the Israelis' access to the sweetest water indicates that the Palestinians and Israelis do not live together peacefully (choice 5).

47. (3) **Comprehension** All that can be inferred from the map and passage is that the West Bank is another settlement area for Palestinians. The passage tells us that the poverty level is lower on the West Bank, which may mean that there is a better water supply and sanitation system (choice 2), but we do not know that for sure. There is no support for the statements concerning the West Bank's importance (choices 1 and 4) or its population (choice 5).

48. (1) **Application** All of the groups but the first would have an interest and motivation for helping those living on the Gaza strip. The Conservation Monitoring Center, however, is an environmental organization whose concern is protecting the land, not helping people to survive on it.

49. (1) **Analysis** The author's tone in this passage is positive. Her enthusiasm for the diversity of living options in Jamaica Plain is evident in the emphasis she places on the community's uniqueness.

50. (5) **Analysis** Only a backwoods recluse who preferred a more rural environment away from other people would not be likely to live in Jamaica Plain.

Power, Authority, and Governance, pages 37–54

1. (1) **Comprehension** The candidate says that he cannot know what he thinks because he does not yet know how the public thinks. This means that some candidates base their opinions on those of the voting public.

2. (3) **Application** If a candidate were to change his mind about a big issue because of public opinion and not because of what he believed was right, then he would be similar to the man in the cartoon.

3. (4) **Application** The power of eminent domain does not allow the government to take property away for any purpose other than for public use.

4. (3) **Analysis** The critics described argue that the regulations take something from landowners. Eminent domain requires the government to pay for what it has taken.

5. (4) **Evaluation** In applying the principle of eminent domain, government officials are allowing the public good to take precedence over the rights of the individual.

6. (3) **Analysis** The response "It's the man who puts money into my pocket that counts" suggests that Democratic leaders have been responsible for improving the economic conditions of minorities.

7. (1) **Evaluation** The statement "It's the man who puts money into my pocket that counts" implies that the voter places a high value on financial security.

8. (4) **Evaluation** Choice (1) is a belief that is used by those opposed to gun control, not those in favor of it. Choice (2) also supports the pro-gun position. Choices (3) and (5) may be facts in favor of gun control, but they do not constitute a legal argument. Only choice (4), with its reference to the Constitutional amendment on the right to bear arms, could be used to support the legal argument for gun control.

9. (4) **Application** Ordained ministers are not prohibited from taking full part in public political life by any U.S. law. All other choices listed have been contested because of the principle of separation of church and state.

10. (4) **Comprehension** Hate speech would be restricted by about 75% of the people who were polled.

11. (2) **Analysis** The author of the passage is emphatic that free speech is absolutely vital for "our system of self-government," which is democracy. Because of free speech, Americans have access to a lot of information and can thus prevent the ignorance that is the "breeding ground for oppression and tyranny."

12. (4) **Application** The researcher who is worried about the connection between pornography and violence would probably be compelled to advocate for controlling pornography, which translates as a restriction on the freedom of speech. The others would all have an interest in seeing that speech is not restricted.

13. (1) **Analysis** Preventing certain classes of people from voting by levying a poll tax presumes that the citizens being denied the vote could not afford to pay the tax. Otherwise, the poll tax requirement would not be an effective barrier to voting.

14. (2) **Analysis** The Fifteenth Amendment precedes the Nineteenth Amendment. Based on this fact, you can conclude that African American men were given the right to vote before women of any color were given the right.

15. (5) **Application** The Twenty-Sixth Amendment gave eighteen-year-olds the right to vote.

16. (4) **Application** The Twenty-Fourth Amendment prohibited the levying of poll taxes that were created to prevent poor whites and African Americans from voting.

17. (5) **Analysis** Only someone who had been born in the United States would not have to apply for permission to work here.

18. (2) **Comprehension** There is no mention on the form for information about previous employers, either in this country or in the applicant's country of origin.

19. (4) **Comprehension** In the top section of the form is a place for INS authorities to check the status of the application. There is no option that mentions the voiding of the application.

20. (3) **Application** Only the factory manager would not be concerned about complying with labor laws if he or she is paying below minimum wage with no employee tracking system. All of the other individuals or organizations would most likely consider themselves obliged to require this documentation of their employees.

21. (5) **Comprehension** According to the passage, Canada once flew the British flag as its own, indicating that country was under British rule. However, today Canada has its own flag as a sign of its independence. Sovereignty means "independence."

22. (4) **Evaluation** The facts that the British Union Jack was Canada's flag and that the Red Ensign incorporated the design support the statement that Canada's historical ties to Great Britain go back many years.

23. (4) **Analysis** The one feature that the five laws have in common is that all, in one way or another, controlled the kind of people who could immigrate to the United States.

24. (3) **Comprehension** A Soviet dissident is an example of a refugee from a communist country. By 1957 the Refugee Relief Act would have been in effect for a few years and could have helped such a person find a home in the United States.

25. (4) **Evaluation** Given that the angry reaction of the people to the brutal attack on "Bloody Sunday" resulted in a shift of power that the Emperor could not have wanted, it is unlikely that the Emperor believed that would happen.

26. (5) **Analysis** *Imperial* refers to someone who assumes supreme authority. The intent of the Constitution, with its concern with checks and balances between the three branches of government, was to prevent the president from becoming "king-like." The president is

to be no more powerful than the Congress or the courts.

27. (2) **Application** George W. Bush's decision to set up military tribunals without first consulting with Congress is most similar to Johnson's and Nixon's decisions to ignore Congress during the Vietnam War. In all of these cases, Congress had not officially declared war, but the President acted as if it had.

28. (3) **Application** Russia was interfering with a Latin American country in placing missiles in Cuba, so it was viewed as an unfriendly act toward the United States. Choices (1), (2), and (4) concerned other countries' internal matters, and choice (5) involved the issue of immigration.

29. (1) **Comprehension** In the Monroe Doctrine the United States declared that it did have a right to extend its authority over the welfare of countries in the Americas.

30. (3) **Application** Only Theodore Roosevelt's proclamation that the United States would intervene in Latin American affairs if Europeans threatened interference was viewed as unfavorable by Latin American governments, since such interference violates the right of self-determination. Choice (1) does not mention Latin America specifically.

31. (4) **Comprehension** The graph shows that more whites voted in the elections over that twenty-year period than either of the other two groups. The graph does not offer any reasons for the difference in group percentages, which rules out choices (1) and (5) and contradicts (2) and (3). In only two years did the percentage of African American voters rise above 50% and it was in 1984, not 1988, that the percentage of African American voters was highest.

32. (5) **Application** The person who would be most concerned about the low voter turnout among minorities is someone who considers minorities to be his or her constituents, or supporters. A candidate whose positions would help minorities would be such a person. The reporter (1) is supposed to be an objective observer, and the Japanese investors would have little interest in who votes, although they might be interested in who wins. Furthermore, the white candidate's supporters are mostly white (2), and the Hispanic congressman has already been elected by white voters (3).

33. (1) **Analysis** Since there was little change in the statistics over a twenty-year period, it is unlikely that they would abruptly change in the next election. Also, the election of George W. Bush, a white Republican, does not support the case for a substantial increase in African American and Hispanic voters, who tend to be Democrats.

34. (3) **Evaluation** Of all the choices listed, only the issue of federally subsidized child day-care centers would not be a priority for the elderly since they are generally beyond the age of needing to care for young children.

35. (5) **Analysis** With this cartoon the artist is illustrating his perception of the potential that 25 million female voters could have on the established political scene, as represented by the donkey (symbol of the Democratic party) and the elephant (symbol of the Republican party).

36. (2) **Comprehension** Wyoming was allowing women to vote as early as 1869. None of the dates on the other states listed precedes 1908.

37. (3) **Evaluation** The newness of the western states and their difference in distance and spirit from the more established and ingrained political views of the rest of the country is the most logical explanation. The people who had crossed the country to settle the West were independent. In addition, women played an important role in the West's settlement.

38. (4) **Analysis** The signs that the men are holding are in many languages, indicating that the people holding them are recent immigrants. The signs that are in English refer to an 8-hour work day and are clearly pro-union, both supporting an interest in improved working conditions for laborers.

39. (4) **Evaluation** Wilson spoke of America as "the example of peace." Even after the sinking of the Lusitania, an event for which a declaration of war would be justified, Wilson refused to retaliate. This indicates that Wilson placed a high value on peace.

40. (5) **Analysis** Choices (1) and (3) are facts, not opinions. Choice (2) is not expressed by the writer, and choice (4) is the opposite of the writer's opinion. The last sentence of the passage expresses the opinion that Wilson was wise not to seek revenge.

41. (4) **Application** Carter chose not to risk a war that might have resulted from attacking Iran. Choices (1), (2), and (3) are not peaceful initiatives. Choice (5) is unrelated to peace or war.

42. (3) **Analysis** Because of the use of "however" and "even so" one can infer that the "plenary power" of the Congress presented a potential threat to the Indians' autonomy. The only option consistent with this understanding is "complete."

43. (4) **Analysis** The passage indicates that there were no significant issues with the Native Americans in the South until Jackson became president. Neither the map nor the passage makes reference to problems the white settlers might have had with their Indian neighbors (1) (2) and (3) or to the degree to which they might have been assimilating within any of the Indian cultures (5). One can only assume, therefore, that whites and the four Indian nations that bordered Alabama were managing to exist peacefully together.

44. (1) **Evaluation** The tone of the passage and the direction in which it suggests the U.S. Government was headed with regard to its treatment of native peoples contradict the suggestion that the tribes' becoming "domestic dependent nations" would ensure their being welcomed as American citizens.

45. (1) **Comprehension** The entire first paragraph emphasizes the irrelevance of the idea of "nation" when considering Asia's past. The second paragraph goes on to describe in more detail how the civilizations of Asia thought of themselves and operated with respect to other groups.

46. (3) **Analysis** The second paragraph describes the process by which China enveloped the Manchu invaders. Therefore, it stands to reason that today there continue to be people in China who can trace their ancestry to those original Manchu nomads.

47. (4) **Comprehension** The author emphasized the irony that this "victory" for the Boy Scouts may not have been a clear victory since it has prompted former Scout supporters to "dissociate" or back away from the organization and to pressure the Scouts to change their policy.

48. (1) **Analysis** The Boy Scouts of America is not a public association and, therefore, is not required by law to include people it doesn't want in its membership. The Supreme Court ruling upheld the right of such private organizations to set their own rules governing who they permit to join their groups.

49. (4) **Comprehension** The striking aspect about the map is how much of the world was touched by the British Empire. No continent was entirely without its influence. The map does indicate, though, that the empire did not stretch into Eastern Europe (1). The passage mentions slavery and trade as major aspects and motivations for the Empire, ruling out choices (2) and (3). Neither the map nor the passage provides information about rebellion within the British colonies (5).

50. (3) **Analysis** Climate would be the only thing that the Empire would not be able to influence within its territories.

Production, Distribution, and Consumption, pages 55–67

1. (1) **Analysis** The last sentence of the passage suggests that labor unions have the power to damage the "struggling economy" of a Third World country.

2. (4) **Analysis** The passage suggests that labor unions in Third World countries like South Korea are working to gain benefits for the workers at the expense of the economy. Choices (1) and (3) are stated in the passage. Choices (2) and (5) are not assumptions that can be made from the passage.

3. (3) **Comprehension** A pigskin is another term for a football. The pigs are labeled "owners" and "players," both of whom are eating from a money-filled trough.

4. (3) **Analysis** Both players and owners are eating as much as they can from a trough of money.

5. (5) **Evaluation** The cartoonist is portraying greed on the parts of the players and owners. A valid conclusion that can be drawn is that both should give in on their demands.

6. (2) **Application** The policy of international corporations hiring cheap foreign labor demonstrates the ideas of domestic jobs being lost and foreign workers being exploited.

7. (3) **Evaluation** The pastoral statement represented a sensitivity toward the needs of the unemployed and the exploited worker; therefore, you could conclude that American Catholic bishops supported the value of economic fairness over private profit.

8. (1) **Application** Only choice (1) demonstrates a foreign investor (Union Carbide), attracted by low wages to an undeveloped country (India), exporting jobs and exploiting workers.

9. (1) **Comprehension** The descriptive terms "smoking entrails," "carcass of the steer," and "steaming hot blood" suggest that Jurgis works in a slaughterhouse.

10. (4) **Evaluation** The excerpt states that Jurgis's "whole soul was dancing with joy—he was at work at last. . . ." This supports the statement that he had been unemployed for a long time.

11. (1) **Analysis** The low wages (17 cents an hour) suggest that the story took place in a very early period. The date 1905 is the only one listed to which this might apply.

12. (2) **Evaluation** A policy of laissez faire in government prohibits in the interference of government in business practices. Each of the reform acts and laws represented greater involvement of the federal government in business.

13. (3) **Application** The Pure Food and Drug Act sets the standards for the production of food and drugs.

14. (4) **Application** Only the Child Labor Laws would have jurisdiction over the employment of those under age fifteen.

15. (2) **Analysis** Only choice (2), which involves a luxury tax, increases the tax burden on the wealthy.

16. (4) **Evaluation** Of the choices listed, only cigarettes are not a necessity of life. Therefore, a tax on cigarettes is the least unfair of the choices listed.

17. (5) **Evaluation** Poor communities are more likely than more affluent ones to have a high percentage of people who are unable to satisfy their survival needs. When a person cannot satisfy survival needs, it is very difficult for that person to focus on other issues, such as elections.

18. (3) **Analysis** The passage states that two or three quarts of water a day is what one human being needs to survive, and that fifty gallons is the amount that some people use. From these facts, you can infer that the author of the passage believes that using fifty gallons of water per day constitutes misuse. All other choices are directly stated in the passage.

19. (2) **Application** It is a paradox that there is a shortage of water when most of the Earth's surface is made up of water.

20. (2) **Application** These countries are like the authoritarian socialist model in which property is public, not private, and individual choice is subordinated to state goals.

21. (5) **Application** Mercantilism emphasizes, among other features, commercial dominance, a goal that can be achieved in part by imposing tariffs on imported goods.

22. (1) **Comprehension** An economy characterized by little or no government intervention is a purely capitalist economy.

23. (4) **Application** Under the sharecropping system, members of the lower class work land owned by a higher class in exchange for shelter and a share of the profits. This system most resembles the manorial feudal system.

24. (4) **Analysis** A cost-of-living adjustment (COLA) is the only means listed by which wages may be kept in line with prices. None of the other choices involve keeping prices and wages parallel.

25. (1) **Analysis** If high unemployment is an indicator of a recession or depression, and high employment is an indicator of a high GNP, it follows that during a recession or depression the GNP would be decreasing.

26. (1) **Comprehension** All of the figures indicate a total debt of more than 100 percent. That means that individual debt exceeded personal income.

27. (2) **Analysis** To decrease the amount of money in circulation during inflationary periods, the Fed would increase the reserve requirement, which would require commercial banks to hold more money and lend less.

28. (5) **Analysis** In order to make a profit, banks must charge higher rates for commercial loans than they have to pay for borrowing money from the Fed. Of the rates listed, only a rate of 12 percent is higher than the 10 percent a member bank would pay.

29. (4) **Evaluation** The only choice that could explain why the DAT recorders did not generate sales is the unavailability of prerecorded DAT tapes. If consumers cannot use an item, little or no market exists for it.

30. (3) **Application** Only choice (3), the failure of Sony's beta-formatted VCR, can be compared to the poor success of the DAT. Despite a reputation for having a sharper picture, the beta-formatted VCR failed largely because of the unavailability of beta videotapes in a market dominated by VHS-formatted VCRs.

31. (4) **Application** A community college's retraining members of the work force would strengthen the trainable work force.

32. (5) **Application** Consumers who put off purchases affect the increase in aggregate demand that is necessary for the economy to grow.

33. (5) **Application** A group that forms a business to help its members save money on groceries would be described as a cooperative.

34. (1) **Application** Only in a sole proprietorship does a single owner have all responsibilities for business debts.

35. (4) **Comprehension** According to the definitions given, in a limited partnership the owners are responsible for business debts only in proportion to the amount they have invested in the business. In a corporation, the individual owners are not personally responsible for the business's debts.

36. (3) **Analysis** According to the figures in the graph, prices continued to rise in spite of the controls.

37. (3) **Analysis** The rate of inflation must have slowed after 1992, since if it had stayed the same, the CPI would have been close to 180 rather than 172.

38. (2) **Comprehension** The CPI measures the price of goods and services. Price and cost mean the same thing.

39. (4) **Comprehension** According to the information provided, only stockholders can vote for the board of directors, the group that officially controls the company and appoints the officers of the company.

40. (4) **Analysis** According to the information in the passage, bond owners' repayments are guaranteed, so they are paid first. While payments to stockholders are made at the discretion of the corporation, preferred stock is guaranteed priority over common stock.

41. (2) **Evaluation** If a state such as Delaware attracts more corporations than any other, the implication is that the corporate climate is better there for those who manage corporations than for individual private investors, because the management determines where a corporation is chartered.

42. (2) **Analysis** The United States entered World War II in 1941. The need for combat aircraft contributed to the increases in revenues for the industry for the years 1941 through 1943.

43. (3) **Evaluation** The fact that the stock price decreased after 1941 (1) was most likely a result of the lower profit, not a cause. It is unlikely that demand for aircraft decreased (4), given the increasing revenue. It is also unlikely that workers were laid off (5), given the increasing revenue and the fact that laying off workers would have increased profit. While it is possible that officials were embezzling funds (2), it is less probable than choice (3). Given the increased production, it is likely that the company hired more workers, and that their profits did not increase in relation to their investment in labor.

44. (2) **Application** The owners are responding to a demand for their product.

45. (1) **Comprehension** The "addictive element" shown in the cartoon is subsidies. The cartoonist suggests that the tobacco companies are addicted to subsidies, just as smokers are addicted to cigarettes.

46. (5) **Analysis** The caption suggests that there are two addictive elements that tobacco companies don't talk about. The most obvious addictive element in tobacco companies' products is nicotine.

47. (4) **Comprehension** A "booming economy" generally refers to high business profits and low unemployment. However, not all workers are benefiting from higher wages during this boom.

48. (1) **Analysis** Most of the new jobs created in recent years have been low-paying work serving the public. By depicting a waitress, the cartoonist shows why those new jobs aren't necessarily benefiting workers.

49. (3) **Comprehension** According to the passage, money experts blamed the stock market collapse on a handful of aggressive young investors who devised a computerized scheme to protect themselves against falling prices.

50. (3) **Comprehension** The total value of equity securities dropped from about 13.5 trillion to 10.6 trillion dollars. This was a loss of more than 20% of the total value of U.S.-headquartered publicly owned companies.

Science, Technology, and Society, pages 69–85

1. (4) **Application** The woman who has a job in IT (Information Technology) and leaves it is reflected in the decreasing numbers of the late 1990s.

2. (4) **Analysis** It is highly unlikely that IT companies consciously decided that they did not want women, and the law would have prohibited companies from openly discriminating on the basis of gender.

3. (3) **Comprehension** Because of the pairing with "pyramid" and the later reference to "massive buildings and monuments," it is reasonable to assume that a ziggurat is most similar to a pyramid. In fact, a ziggurat is a triangular temple, like the pyramid, but with terraced walls rather than smooth ones.

4. (1) **Comprehension** Although it is clear from the passage that many workers were engaged in the construction of the ziggurats and pyramids, the passage does not state or imply that it was with those civilizations that slavery began.

5. (1) **Analysis** Since much of rural Chile had never before had electricity at all, even a small amount of power would have been welcome. Cost of parts, ease of transportation and repair, and availability of energy source, however, would have been significant determining factors.

6. (4) **Evaluation** The only conclusion that is supported by the information provided concerns reading, even though one cannot precisely determine which reason would account for the small percentage of people who use electricity to facilitate their reading.

7. (2) **Analysis** The passage gives repeated examples of the Soviets preceding the Americans in accomplishing their goals.

8. (3) **Evaluation** The author implies that the American public was more impressed with the Soviets' speed than with the United States's plans and perseverance.

9. (5) **Analysis** The entire passage emphasizes the Soviets' ability to upstage the United States by preceding it in making technological advances. Choice (5) is the only choice listed that reflects this emphasis.

10. (3) **Evaluation** The focus of this picture is the child. Someone who was advocating for the rights of children might have used this picture to change the labor laws in order to protect a girl like the one in the picture from long hours of work in an unhealthy environment, which likely kept her from school.

11. (5) **Comprehension** The second sentence states that the Anglo-Saxons didn't make the connection between germs, which they thought of as the weapons of elves, and infection. The rest of the paragraph describes how their method of treatment of infection was far removed from its true cause.

12. (4) **Application** Antibiotics are what modern medical science has developed to counter infection. The role of an antibiotic, like that of the elf arrow, is to kill the germ causing the infection.

13. (2) **Evaluation** In this passage there is an interesting mix of references to both a pagan view ("elves," "sprites," and spells) and a Judeo-Christian one (the devil and the Lord). At the end, however, the reference to paganism is made with a cautionary tone, inferring that it was considered more appropriate to use language more consistent with the Judeo-Christian view than the pagan.

14. (1) **Analysis** Given the number of vaccines recommended and the number of times a vaccine needs to be administered in order to immunize a child successfully, regular visits to a doctor are necessary.

15. (4) **Analysis** Access to doctors and medicines such as vaccines is part of the criteria for determining a country's standard of living. Because it is clear that fully immunizing a child requires a high degree of access to medical care, one can infer that fewer children in countries with less access would be immunized.

16. (2) **Analysis** The fact that George Washington needed false teeth is not likely to have had a significant impact on future events. The other historical events, however, had a large impact on many people.

17. (5) **Evaluation** The focus of the cartoon is American history and the potential impact that a handheld computer might have had on a handful of events. The humor derives from actually depicting the way in which certain events in America might have been different had there been handheld computers available.

18. (2) **Comprehension** The passage does not describe how the first printing press was designed. The machine it refers to is the "new" and faster press made possible by the steam engine.

19. (1) **Comprehension** The passage emphasizes that the scarce resource was readers.

20. (4) **Application** The Industrial Revolution, which involved the development of efficient machines and made possible the mass production of goods, would have included the rotary-driven steam press.

21. (3) **Evaluation** The author states that the result of the combination of the steam engine and the printing press was as "explosive" as that of the computer and the telephone. He then goes on to discuss the significant changes brought about by the steam press. While choice (1) is true, it is not the reason for the comparison. There is no information in the passage to support choices (2), (4), and (5).

22. (3) **Analysis** The only possibility that is consistently supported by the passage is the settlement of humans near sources of water. The passage mentions two river settlements, one on the Canadian River and the other along the Pecos River, as well as a settlement along the coast of the Gulf of Mexico.

23. (2) **Application** Ceremonial cannibalism, which involved the sacrificing and eating of fellow humans, is an example of a practice that would be highly unlikely to have required technology or contributed to its advancement.

24. (1) **Analysis** The Latinos pictured in the cartoon are farm workers and, therefore, not likely to have the money to buy a computer, let alone use the Internet. Farm workers generally earn very low wages and often move frequently while living under substandard conditions.

25. (4) **Analysis** In the cartoon, the pollster is asking if the farm workers use the Internet, but they think he is referring to the nets they are wearing. Therefore, you can infer that they are probably not familiar with the Internet. There is no information to support choices (1) and (2), and while (3) and (5) are elements of the cartoon, they are not the basis for its humor.

26. (4) **Application** The graph reveals that it takes a significant period of time (approximately two years) for an inexperienced worker to reach a high speed of production. This data could be used to support the efforts of the manager who advocates keeping experienced workers over hiring new ones.

27. (3) **Evaluation** The only choice that may be both correctly inferred from the graph and considered an advantage is the fact that machines begin production at an efficient level and can maintain that level.

28. (3) **Analysis** The second sentence states that many believe that a representative government is the "only form of democracy" that is feasible in today's large countries of diverse populations. This leads to the logical assumption that there are many such countries and, thus, many such governments.

29. (1) **Evaluation** The tone that the author of the passage takes is generally supportive of direct citizen involvement in government decision making. By mentioning how elected officials are "squandering" their power, he is emphasizing how people taking the "power over their own lives and goods" is a positive option.

30. (4) **Comprehension** The end of the passage emphasizes that the discovery of ether is a victory for all nations and for people now and in the future.

31. (2) **Application** All of the events or periods listed precede 1847 except the American Civil War. Ether would prove to be extremely helpful in treating the wounded in that war.

32. (5) **Application** Like the nuclear-energy accident, the atomic bomb was the result of human invention. Both nuclear energy and the atomic bomb involve advanced scientific understanding, and both emit extremely toxic radiation.

33. (1) **Application** The cleaning crew members most likely would have worn protective suits, knowing they were going into a radioactive area. However, none of the other choices would have been protected in that way, either at the time of the explosion or in the days, weeks, and months following it.

34. (2) **Evaluation** The passage mentions the Greeks' and Romans' understandings and inventions of such things as fossil fuels and interchangeable parts that turned out to be critical to the Industrial Revolution. The Greek and Roman societies existed in the early centuries of the Common Era (C.E.), long before 1800.

35. (4) **Analysis** Antibiotics are a medical breakthrough that would have had little to no impact on technological progress as referred to in the passage.

36. (5) **Application** Sub-Saharan Africa is an area of the world with an extremely poor rural population, similar to that of ancient Greece and Rome. The other choices are considered part of the "developed" or technologically advanced world with high standards of living.

37. (3) **Analysis** Because of the increased number of mills evident in the map from 1836, it is logical that there would also be an increase in pollution (1), workers (2), housing for the workers (4) and economic dependence on the business generated by the mills (5). Only the stance of politicians cannot be determined from the change in the maps.

38. (5) **Analysis** Mills depended upon water as a source of power. This would have been true of mills in other areas as well as in Pawtucket.

39. (3) **Comprehension** The ovals hold the place of each institution in the epochs that follow the institutions' initial development.

40. (4) **Comprehension** In the current epoch there are five ovals and one square, signifying the new institution of this epoch (the Internet) (1). This totals six. The diagram does not indicate that any of the institutions, including religion, are failing (3) and one of the main points of the diagram is to demonstrate how all institutions can be traced back to the beginning (5).

41. (3) **Application** The American Revolution was an example of a democratic revolution, a phenomenon that the diagram locates within CivIII.

42. (5) **Application** The kinds of changes in each of the institutions of Civ IV were the result in large part of rapid developments in technology. Those institutions and their changes continued into CivV, together with the introduction of the Internet, an indisputable result of technological advancement.

43. (4) **Evaluation** The connections between epochs that clearly lead back to a single source are evident in the structure of the diagram.

44. (1) **Application** Only the field-tested drug meets the patent criteria described in the passage. Faraday's discovery (2) is an example of a scientific principle. The revised and improved software (3) is an example of a change to a previously known invention. A novel (4) would be granted a copyright, not a patent; and a security system desensitizer (5) would be used for illegal purposes.

45. (2) **Evaluation** The common aspect of all inventions is that they are the product of an individual's or group's creativity, which is the ability to make something new. Intellectual property laws in the U.S. supports that ability by giving creators the right to financially benefit from their creations.

46. (4) **Comprehension** By capitalizing the letters in the word "such" the cartoonist is emphasizing the excitement around the connection of the two railroad lines. The word "amends," however, suggests that there had been difficulties in the process of making the achievement.

47. (5) **Analysis** It is doubtful that the railroad companies would have persevered with their project if they had thought that most people would be unable to afford to make use of the transcontinental line. All of the other options are likely results of completing the railroad.

48. (2) **Analysis** Africa, Latin America, and the Caribbean are regions with developing countries. The shocking discrepancy between the data-carrying capability of those areas and of the other regions of the world that are so much more developed, at least partly explains why those areas have not kept up technologically.

49. (3) **Comprehension** Classism refers to the disdain and prejudice that one social class (usually higher) has for another (usually lower). The distinction that the Renaissance made between science and technology (gentile vs. vulgar) was a clear-cut example of this disdain and prejudice. Racism (1) refers to negative feelings and behaviors of one race (usually a majority) toward another (usually a minority) and sexism (2) of one gender (usually male) toward the other (usually female). Xenophobia (4) is a fear of foreigners and homophobia (5) is a fear of homosexuals.

50. (2) **Analysis** Because of the reference at the end of the paragraph to the eventual development of an urban, mercantile economy, one can conclude that prior to that time the economy would have been the opposite (rural based and agricultural).

Global Connections, pages 87–106

1. (4) **Application** The Vietcong had fewer resources, fewer soldiers, less food, and lower pay than the Americans during the Vietnam War but won the war.

2. (4) **Comprehension** According to the passage, the Americans defeated Great Britain, which is described as the greatest superpower at that time in history.

3. (5) **Analysis** The passage states that "Japan will never again wage war against other countries or even maintain an army, navy, or air force." From this we can infer that Japan does not pay to support armed forces.

4. (1) **Application** A dictator is a powerful chief executive. If Germany and Italy feared the return of dictatorships, their governments would have limited the executive branch.

5. (3) **Analysis** The entire passage describes the influence of the U.S. Constitution around the world. None of the other opinions could be supported by the information provided.

6. (2) **Application** Shutting down the production of periodicals (magazines) contradicts the ideal of freedom of the press. Choices (1) and (3) allow more freedoms; choices (4) and (5) do not involve ideals cited in the passage.

7. (2) **Comprehension** The excerpt begins by describing the scenario of what would happen if the United States went bankrupt. Therefore, you can infer that the author is referring to the United States when he describes its economy as the most powerful on the face of the Earth.

8. (3) **Analysis** The passage states that in the event of a default by the United States, "The dollar would drop so low that even the Democratic Republic of the Congo wouldn't buy it." This implies that the Congo is a poor nation. However, not enough information is provided for you to conclude that the Congo is the poorest nation on Earth.

9. (5) **Analysis** The passage states that the sale of militarily sensitive electronic products to foreign countries is forbidden. The only party listed that is connected directly to the military is the Pentagon.

10. (1) **Analysis** Of all three trade groups, Canada shows the least variation in the value of its trade balance with the United States. A relatively even line indicates consistency.

11. (4) **Comprehension** Dollar figures were lower in 1992 than in 1983, so the overall balance declined. Figures rose between 1987 and 1990, so the decline wasn't steady.

12. (2) **Evaluation** The U.S. balance of trade with all three groups fell. That means that the value of U.S. exports minus imports was lower than in the previous year. Such a drop could only happen if the United States exported fewer goods and/or imported more.

13. (2) **Analysis** The area of greatest concentration of Hispanics extends along the entire Mexico-United States border from California to Texas. Southern and Central California is just part of that area.

14. (3) **Evaluation** Given the high percentage of Hispanics in El Paso and the importance of English in the United States, it would make most sense to increase funding for ESOL classes. Because so many residents of El Paso are Hispanic, it would be discriminatory to restrict the public use of Spanish and misguided to discontinue Spanish instruction in the schools. Given El Paso's proximity to Mexico, it would also be wise to encourage, not discourage, instruction in Mexican history and culture.

15. (5) **Evaluation** Circumvent means to go around. The Nazis went around the forts of the Maginot Line by invading France via Belgium. There were no forts on the French-Belgian border.

16. (5) **Analysis** The photo clearly shows that for a national leader, Gandhi lived extremely simply and humbly.

17. (5) **Comprehension** According to the chart, used engine oil from road runoff and oil changes is by far the greatest source of oil released into the environment, making it the greatest threat to the environment.

18. (1) **Application** Recycling used oil from vehicle oil changes would probably have the greatest effect on reducing the amount of oil released into the environment, because it would address the largest problem, the accumulation of used engine oil from road runoff and oil changes.

19. (4) **Application** Since NAFTA Man needs to commute from the United States to Mexico every day, he would be most likely to support increased funding for more border crossings into Mexico.

20. (4) **Analysis** NAFTA Man is most similar to a resident of the Netherlands who works in Belgium and is comfortable with the languages and cultures of both countries. Both have learned to function well in two cultures. Both also live in free-trade zones. The resident of the Netherlands can easily work in Belgium because of the economic policies of the European Union.

21. (2) **Application** According to the information in this passage, a new steel mill would not be the type of project that should be supported. All of the other programs are important, but the seed-distribution and farmer-training program would probably have the greatest long-term impact for improving conditions in the country.

22. (4) **Application** The Gulf War, in which a coalition of forces led by the United States drove Saddam Hussein's army out of Kuwait, is the only example that does not follow the pattern described in the article. Iraq had invaded Kuwait in order to acquire its huge oil deposits. The United States led a large coalition that decisively defeated Hussein's army in a battle known as Desert Storm.

23. (3) **Analysis** A rock is not likely to damage a tank or divert it from a target. The only reasonable explanation is that they were expressing rage and frustration at the Soviet invasion.

24. (1) **Analysis** All of the choices are reasons the photograph is shocking. However, what is most shocking about this image is the use of the American flag, the symbol of democracy and freedom, as a weapon of hate and bigotry.

25. (3) **Analysis** Although we might suspect that the photographer might be sympathetic to the integration of the Boston Public Schools, we can make a stronger argument that the photographer was realizing the importance of documenting this attack. He was putting himself at some risk by being so close and photographing this violent incident. This photograph was an extremely negative image for Boston.

26. (3) **Evaluation** The sleek, stark, bold lines of the sculpture and building appear to be promoting and valuing the concepts of modernity and progress above all else. The scale is monumental rather than human, the image is cold and formal, and there is no hint that this country has millions of desperately poor citizens. The structures are built in an international style that is entirely disconnected from Brazil's heritage.

27. (1) **Analysis** The image powerfully conveys the suffering and deprivation caused by war.

28. (2) **Evaluation** The information in the passage illustrates that Leopold's troops would rather mutilate a human being than be called to account for "wasting" a bullet. There is no evidence in the passage that the soldiers valued the lives of the Congolese. Even their productivity could not have been valued since many of them were mutilated.

29. (4) **Comprehension** The passage states that half the population, or 8 to 10 million people, died during Leopold's rule. If half the populations was 8 to 10 million, then the entire population in 1880 must have been about 18 million.

30. (3) **Analysis** The conclusion that can be drawn is that the Belgians tried to cover up the extent of the abuses in the Congo. The other choices are facts that support that conclusion.

31. (5) **Evaluation** According to the passage, the Clintons are in front of a huge crowd in Ghana. They are standing with hands clasped and upraised with Jerry Rawlings, the President of Ghana. This pose is one of solidarity. By wearing the traditional cloth of Ghana, the Clintons most likely were trying to emphasize their closeness to the people of Ghana and respect for their culture.

32. (1) **Comprehension** The main point of this cartoon is that aid must travel through a difficult maze to get to the recipient. By the time it travels through that maze, not much is left.

33. (4) **Analysis** Cutting red tape for organizations that can provide and deliver aid would most directly address the problem of getting aid to recipients as quickly and efficiently as possible.

34. (4) **Application** The childhood home of Abraham Lincoln was a modest structure. All of the other choices are beautiful monumental structures that have a positive impact on the viewer similar to the impact of the United States Capitol.

35. (2) **Comprehension** The passage states that Lincoln wanted the dome completed as a symbol of the permanence of the Union.

36. (2) **Evaluation** According to the article, the key cause of the problem is consumers who value getting a bargain price more than anything else.

37. (3) **Analysis** The passage makes it clear that the filmmakers Woods and Blewett are strongly opposed to child slave labor. Therefore, they would be most likely to support boycotting companies that market products manufactured through child slave labor.

38. (4) **Analysis** The map shows the world from 705–500 B.C. At that time the ancient Greeks were colonizing the Mediterranean Sea and Black Sea, and agricultural communities, or agrarian societies, were developing in Central and South America, as can be seen from the descriptions of the crops growing there.

39. (3) **Evaluation** Most of the developed area are either on or near a coastline or along a major river.

40. (5) **Analysis** The photograph provides ample proof that modern development has not yet come to this portion of the Sahara. Commerce is still being carried on by camel caravan, as it has been for hundreds of years.

41. (2) **Analysis** Since the image is so starkly beautiful, most likely the photographer had great respect for what he was photographing. There is no hint of contempt for what is being depicted, or any particular opinions about the workers or animals. And because this is a recent picture showing an ongoing trade, it would not be considered nostalgic for something that has already disappeared.

42. (2) **Evaluation** This billboard in China is promoting the one-child policy. The purpose of the policy was to reduce the rate of population increase in order to increase the standard of living for all Chinese.

43. (3) **Analysis** Both the cartoon and the graph clearly show that population growth is a major issue for poor, developing countries. Choices (1), (2), and (5) can only be determined from the graph, while choice (4) could only be determined from the cartoon.

44. (2) **Comprehension** The artist makes it clear that what is keeping poor countries down is overpopulation, or too many people.

45. (3) **Evaluation** Spain is the only country shown that was an Islamic country during the time period shown on the map, but is not today. Iran and Morocco were Islamic then and still are today, and Russia and Tibet were not Islamic then, nor are they now.

46. (4) **Comprehension** While the Vikings were crossing the North Atlantic during the period depicted in the map, they had not yet converted to Christianity.

47. (3) **Evaluation** Given the research and development taking place throughout Asia, it is likely that some alternatives to crude oil will be developed and marketed. Because they are still being developed, it is not possible to conclude that these sources will replace crude oil as the main source of energy (2), that these sources will control pollution (4), or that Asia will become the leading producer of these sources of energy. The passage contradicts the idea that there will be a push to find new oil fields, at least in Asia.

48. (1) **Comprehension** This passage is about Asian nations exploring alternative energy sources to reduce energy imports and pollution.

49. (3) **Analysis** Americans have often thought that they were immune from attack. The terrorist attack against the World Trade Center in New York and the Pentagon near Washington, D.C. made clear that we were no more protected than anyone else. (1) and (2) are incorrect because the continents did not actually move and America is still physically separate from the Eastern Hemisphere. (4) is incorrect because the time is the time of the attack on the United States, not our military response to the attack. (5) is incorrect because there is no implication in the cartoon that we will always be under threat from terrorists, just that the world is a much more interconnected place than we had previously realized.

50. (2) **Analysis** Rather than focusing on the horror of the terrorist attack, the cartoonist emphasizes how the attack has brought Americans closer to other people around the world. One important aspect of that closeness is the empathy people everywhere felt for Americans.